Profiles in Black

Profiles in Black

Edited by Doris Funnye Innis
Juliana Wu
Consulting Editor: Joyce Duren

**Biographical Sketches of 100 Living
Black Unsung Heroes**

First Edition

CORE Publications, a division of the Congress of Racial Equality

New York, 1976

Copyright © 1976 by CORE Publications, a division of the Congress of Racial Equality. All rights reserved. No part of this book may be reproduced or transmitted in any form or by any means, electronic or mechanical, including photocopying, recording, or any information storage and retrieval system, without written permission in writing from the publisher. Manufactured in the United States of America.

Library of Congress Catalog Card Number 76-27634

Library of Congress Cataloging in Publication Data

Profiles in Black.

    Bibliography: p. 232
    Includes index.
    1. Afro-Americans—Biography. I. Innis, Doris Funnye.
II. Duren, Joyce. III. Wu, Juliana.
E185.96.P76   920'.073   76-27634
ISBN 0-917354-01-X

Book design by Al Green

Picture Credits

E.J. Anderson by Taylor Made Photographers; V.R. Anderson by Sky Lite Studio; M.R. Brown by George W. Martin; J.A. Childs III by Page Studio; J.R. Doman, Jr. by Becket Logan; J. Galvin-Lewis by Laima Turnley; B. Gilliam by EGR Travel International Inc.; E.T. Graham by Miami-Metro Department of Publicity and Tourism; T.J. Haig with permission of the *Providence Journal Bulletin*; A. Hansen by Austin Victor Hansen; R.B. Harris courtesy of the National Aeronautics and Space Administration; A. Hollingsworth by Earl Fowler; E.C. Jenkins by George Frye; A.G. Kearney by Ronald Simmons; E.S. Kinney by Austin Hansen; N. Long by Oscar Productions Inc.; C.L. Montgomery by the City of San Diego; H. O'Bryant by Nolan Davis; B.S. Preiskel by Blackstone-Shelburne; C. Rainey III by Kenneth Peterson; E.C. Reid by Gill Photographers; C.M. Reynolds, Jr. by Arthur "Bud" Smith; N. Russell by Gabusi Studio; J. Shern by Herb Shoebridge; V. Smith courtesy of the Larcada Gallery, New York; T. Thomas by Charles T. Garrett; L.C. Tombs courtesy of the Dept. of Agriculture, Office of Minority Business Enterprise; C. Tonic by Leonard Jackson; B. Walker by Stuart Leffler; D. Wethers by A. McGowan; J.J. Williams by W.C. Baker; N. Williams by Gaffney Photography.

To all Black youths who *can* and *would* if we will show them the way
To Edward W. Blyden, Martin Delany, Marcus Garvey, Roy Innis, and other leaders who have shown the way

Ambition is the desire to go forward and improve one's condition. It is a burning flame that lights up the life of the individual and makes him see himself in another state. To be ambitious is to be great in mind and soul. To want that which is worthwhile and strive for it. To go on without looking back, reaching to that which gives satisfaction....
(1923)
—*Marcus Garvey*

Acknowledgments

The editors wish to gratefully acknowledge the splendid cooperation of the persons profiled in this book; the organizations, associations, groups and countless individuals who responded to our requests for nominees: Mr. and Mrs. Wilson Phelps for their initial aid at the start of this project; Charles Cook for his coordination with the West Coast promotional and editorial aspects involving this book; Eleanor Hurka, librarian at the Minority Business Information Institute, for her patient and fruitful research; and Denise Mitchell for her initial research and continual cooperation and interest in this project. The editors also acknowledge with gratitude permission to reprint passages or lines that appear within these pages: John A. Williams for a quote from *This is My Country Too*. Permission granted by the author; all rights reserved by the author; Grove Press for a statement from *The Autobiography of Malcolm X*, reprinted by permission of Grove Press, Inc., from the book entitled *The Autobiography of Malcolm X* by Malcolm X with the assistance of Alex Haley. Copyright 1964 by Alex Haley and Malcolm X. Copyright 1965 by Alex Haley and Betty Shabazz; Beacon Press for a passage from James Baldwin's *Notes of a Native Son*. Copyright 1955 by James Baldwin; *The Nation* for a statement from an article by Langston Hughes that appeared in its pages in 1926.

Preface

We want to tell you a story—a true story, mind you—about a young Black girl who grew up in a map-less Southern town. Her name does not matter; that she was Black does. Her hunger, her thirst for knowledge was unrelenting; it plagued her night and day.

This young girl had great fun growing up—doing the things that are uniquely southern. But all the while her active mind yearned for experiences that would satisfy her hunger, her thirst. She wanted to be a writer but she was rebuffed and discouraged at every turn. "What? A writer! *What* will you do?" asked one classmate who thought this searching soul was quite out of her mind.

Profiles in Black was conceived, therefore, primarily as encouragement and inspiration to such a girl and all other Black boys and girls (in both the North and South) who were told that this, that and the other was "out." This book seeks to make one correct step in reversing existing patterns. The publisher and editors feel that a Black youth should be given every encouragement in the direction that he or she is inclined, and if he or she has the suitable potential for a particular career; not to be told by a programmed, misguided (read "racist") guidance counselor, "Oh, you'll never make it at such and such; why not do so and so?" It is a wide, wide world out there and we want our youths—the salvation of our race—to know about it.

This book is intended to be used in schools, libraries and by the general public. It consists of biographical profiles of 100 living Black men and women —from Logan, Utah, to New York City—who have made their marks in their chosen fields and who—despite sometimes overwhelming obstacles (invariably related to being Black)—have made remarkable strides in their chosen endeavors and have in turn utilized their achievements to service and inspire the Black community. The names of the individuals profiled are not household words except, perhaps, in their particular community or region. They are in a sense unsung heroes and heroines.

The concept of *Profiles in Black* seemed simple enough, but its execution proved to be nothing short of a massive detective search. Literally hundreds upon hundreds of organizations and associations—religious, secular, business, civic, fraternal—were contacted and asked to recommend worthy individuals. Upon their recommendations, the editors contacted numerous individuals and perused many library collections. Letters, repeated phone calls, legwork—all were utilized in this search. The result is that close to a hundred professions and sub-professions are represented in this book.

Many individuals were not profiled here, however, due to limitations of time and space—a fact regretted by the editors.

It is a matter of great concern to the publisher and editors that so many Black youths see no one to emulate; nothing to aspire to. Black youths do not relate *actively* to dead heroes and they find it difficult to relate to many of our present leaders. Not since the Reconstruction period in the history of our country have we had so many leaders—both elected and self-appointed. But the vast majority of Black youth cannot relate to them because they do not look like them. If a youth is Black-skinned and has kinky hair but his congressman's hair is straight (or what is called "good") and his complexion is fair, it is wrenching—if not impossible—for the youth to relate to that congressman, that leader, or to relate to him as a "spokesman" for Black people. By dress, by various methods of denaturing oneself, by contorted speech, Black youths can try to imitate—but can *never* identify. This is a matter of deep seriousness that has crippled our youths for generations. It is time to call a halt.

The editors have taken every care to make this book as accurate as possible; however, any failing is completely assumed by the editors.

—The Editors

A Note from the Publisher

The most debilitating form of racism in America is that of intra-racial discrimination and prejudice. Historically, wherever the Black man has found himself oppressed, a hybrid class has developed, comprised of the offspring of Blacks and their oppressors. This class hardens into a caste, when they marry only among themselves to perpetuate their kind. This caste is used as a buffer by the oppressor. Even after the oppressor is expelled, the problem persists—in fact, our liberation is always thwarted by the existence of this phenomenon.

—Roy Innis

Contents

Acknowledgments 6

Preface 7

Profiles 12

Source List 232

Index 238

It seemed to me a great hardship that I was born poor, and it seemed an even greater hardship that I should have been born a Negro. I did not like to admit, even to myself, that I felt this way about the matter, because it seemed to me an indication of weakness and cowardice for any man to complain about the condition he was born to. Later I came to the conclusion that it was not only weak and cowardly, but that it was a mistake to think of the matter in the way in which I had done. I came to see that, along with his disadvantages, the Negro in America had some advantages, and I made up my mind that opportunities that had been denied him from without could be more than made up by greater concentration and power within. (1911)

—Booker T. Washington
Educator, College President

Airline Pilot
WILLIAM NORWOOD
Chicago, Illinois

William Norwood received his inspiration for flying from his elementary school principal who was a member of the all-Black 99th Pursuit Squadron in World War II. Norwood asserts that he prepared himself for his career in aviation by becoming more competitive and seeking new challenges. He was the first Black quarterback on both his high school and college teams. He received his private pilots's license during his senior year at Southern Illinois University in June 1959.

While he was playing quarterback in one of the games, his older sister was watching and heard one spectator remark, "They have niggers playing quarterback—pretty soon they'll be flying airplanes." Norwood says, "This comment did wonders for my resolve. Early in life I realized the extra effort needed for a Black to succeed and survive."

Upon his graduation, he received pilot training while in the Air Force. He was counseled not to request assignment to a particular air base because no Black pilots had ever graduated from there, but he was stubborn and did graduate. He flew B-52s in the Air Force for six years.

When the airlines began to open opportunities for employment in the mid-sixties, Norwood joined United Airlines as their first Black pilot in 1965. In March 1974, he obtained a Master's in business administration at the University of Chicago.

In 1974, Norwood was appointed by Gov. Dan Walker of Illinois as a member of the board of trustees at Southern Illinois University. Norwood is a member of the Aviation Board of Elk Grove Villiage, Illinois. He spends time giving motivational speeches to inner-city classes about aviation.

His philosophy and advice is "to work hard and success will come because now most things are possible. Most important, aim for excellence and give your best to every job you attempt."

Medical Educational Director
DOROTHY LAVINIA BROWN
Nashville, Tennessee

Dorothy Lavinia Brown was the first Black woman surgeon in the South. She never knew her father until she was at the height of her career. Born in Philadelphia, she lived in the Troy orphans' home in Troy, New York, from five months until she was 12½ years old. She received her grade school and high school education in Troy and obtained her Bachelor of Arts degree at Bennett College, Greensboro, North Carolina (1941), and her Doctor of Medicine degree from Meharry Medical College, Nashville, Tennessee (1948). During all of her educational career she worked, starting at age 14 as a part-time maid and in laundry and dry cleaning work in Albany, New York; she was engaged in doing "daywork" in Troy; and she was an inspector with the Rochester Army Ordnance after college.

After medical school Dr. Dorothy Brown did her internship at Harlem Hospital in New York from 1948-49 and her residency as an attending surgeon at George W. Hubbard Hospital from 1949-54 in Nashville, Tennessee. Thereafter, she became chief of surgery at Riverside Hospital, Nashville, Tennessee (1957 to the present). She was invited to be clinical professor of surgery at Meharry Medical College in 1965. Dr. Brown then became Director of Student Health Service at Fisk-Meharry from 1971-73. She is currently the educational director of the Meharry-Riverside Clinical Rotation Program.

In 1968, as the first Black woman to serve as a State Representative in the Tennessee Legislature, Dr. Brown initiated and sponsored a bill which came to within two votes of being passed to revise the abortion ruling in Tennessee. She would like to run again for the legislature to pass a bill in regard to the National Health Insurance Plan.

In addition to her numerous honorary memberships, Dr. Brown is a Fellow of the American College of Medicine, and is a member of the Nashville Academy of Medicine, the R. F. Boyd Medical Society, the National Medical Association and Religious and Professional Organizations. She was on the Governor's Commission on the Status of Women (1972-73), and fulfilled one term on the board of directors of the Nashville Area Chamber of Commerce. She also holds a number of awards and citations: three awards for outstanding achievements from Delta Sigma Theta Sorority (1963), as an outstanding citizen from the Davidson County Business and Professional Women's Club (1966-67). She was voted Woman of the Year by the Nashville Jaycees (1967). Meharry Medical College named the Women's Building after Dorothy L. Brown (1970). Dr. Brown received an honorary Doctor of Science degree from Russell Sage College, Troy, New York (1972).

Dr. Dorothy Brown has written articles for the *Journal of the National Medical Association* and for the *Southern Medical Journal*.

Dr. Brown advises that "although it is more difficult for women to get training in surgery programs, it can be done."

Profiles in Black

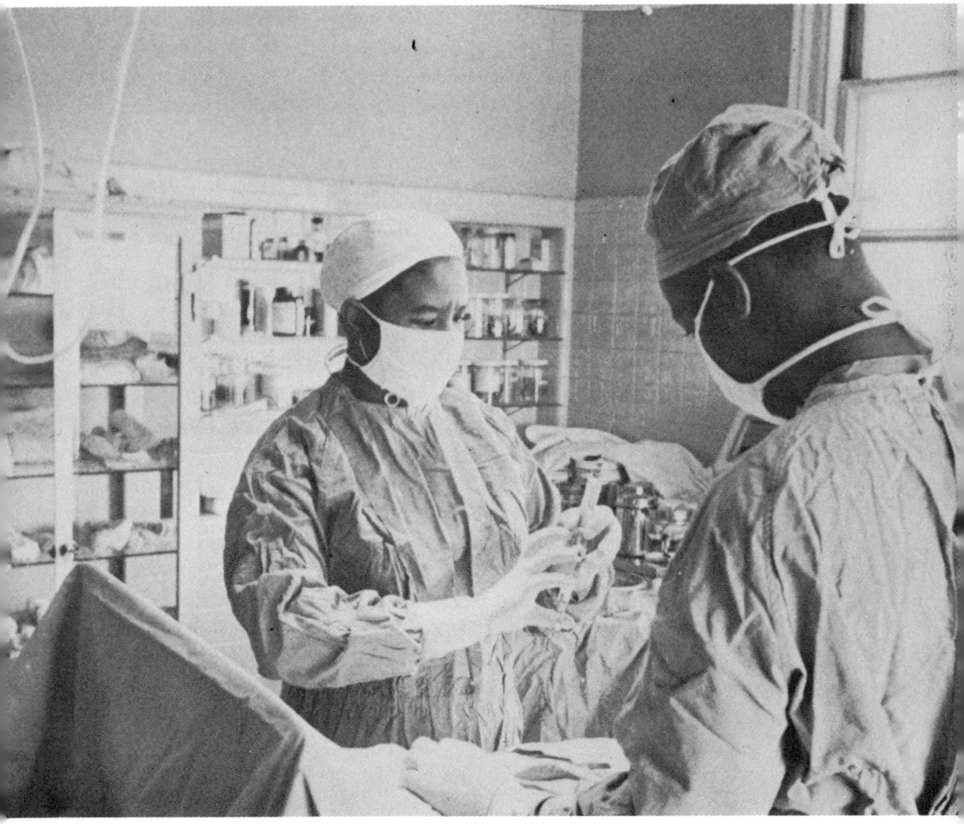

15

16

Science Educator
ARCHIE LACEY
New York, New York

Archie Lacey, the 13th of 16 children, was born in 1923 in a small coal-mining town, Boothton, Alabama, 30 miles outside of Birmingham. After grade school, Lacey had to attend the segregated County Training School, which was 33 miles away and three "white schools" past his house. He made the 66-mile trip to school every day, graduating as valedictorian of his class in 1940.

He attended Alabama State Teachers College for the next three years. In 1943, he served with the U.S. Army Corps of Engineers. After his term of service he attended Howard University as a special graduate student in chemistry from 1948-49. After pursuing those studies he became a science instructor at Alabama State Branch Junior College, Mobile, from 1949-52.

He studied at Northwestern University, Evanston, Illinois, for three years, obtaining his Master's degree in 1953 and his doctorate in education in 1955. He served as science education instructor ar the same university in the summer of 1955. He then became associate professor of science at Alabama State College, Montgomery, from 1955-57. From 1957-60, he was professor of physical sciences at Grambling College in Louisiana.

In 1960, Archie Lacey was invited to join the faculty of Hunter College as assistant professor and was promoted to associate professor in 1964. He became the first Black male professor to receive tenure at Hunter College in New York City.

In 1968, he was invited to join the staff of Herbert H. Lehman College, also in New York City, and was promoted to full professor a year later. In 1969, he took a one-year leave of absence to establish the Division of Education at the Federal City College of Washington, D.C. In 1972, he was elected chairman of the Department of Education at Lehman College.

A well-recognized national leader in science education, Prof. Lacey has written many articles and two books, *Chemistry of Life* and *Guide to Science Teaching*. He has served as consultant for many private and government educational agencies.

In 1974, Prof. Lacey was selected as one of eight distinguished alumni to graduate from Alabama State College during its centenary year.

Prof. Lacey is married, and he and his wife have four children.

Profiles in Black

Trainer Consultant
JANE GALVIN-LEWIS
New York, New York

Jane Galvin-Lewis is the co-director and co-founder, along with Carol Shapiro, of Social Change Advocates, an organization established in 1974 to "alleviate and prevent the damaging effects of racism and sexism, both oppressive forces which we feel imperative to work toward their elimination...." The multi-racial staff of the organization offers workshops and training sessions in non-sexist, multi-racial and multi-cultural context; they have developed educational materials such as toys and puzzles to "enhance the self-image of each child in the classroom"; and designed a freer, more conducive learning environment; and they offer consultation as well as the workshops and training sessions in race relations and sexism in their affirmative-action cirriculum.

Ms. Galvin-Lewis feels that racism and sexism are derived from the same seed. To fight these two oppressions, she believes, people can be trained to overcome fears by the preparation of taking responsibility to create changes. She has promoted this training through her lectures at numerous colleges and universities and through her work at Haryou-Act and her work as housing coordinator for unwed mothers and as the national program director of Dahomey, West Africa, where she taught English and economics for two years.

Her career in the United States has been equally extensive, beginning as a Freedom Rider in the Sixties and later as a field worker with the Associated Community Teams in Harlem, New York, in 1963; as the district advisor at the Greater Essex County Council in Orange, New Jersey, specializing in the inner-city community organizations from 1963-66; as an instructor at South Hampton College of Long Island University in 1966; as trainer/consultant for Volt Technical Information Sciences from 1968-70; and the Mount Vernon Community Action Group from 1967-70. Ms Galvin-Lewis was also national program coordinator of the National Council of Negro Women for one year in 1970 and deputy director of the Women's Action Alliance.

Currently, she is an instructor at the Sagaris Institute on Women in Lindenville, Vermont.

Among her many affiliations are memberships of the Chancellor's Advisory Commission to Eliminate Sex Discrimination in New York City Public Schools, the National Black Feminist Organization, of which she is a founding member; the New York State Human Rights Commission; the National Council of Negro Women; the Coalition of 100 Black Women; the Manhattan Women's Political Caucus.

Ms. Galvin-Lewis was born in Ithaca, New York, and did her undergraduate work at Boston University in the social sciences and received her Master's degree at New York University in 1963. She has done some doctoral work at Columbia University, New York City.

Profiles in Black

19

Photographer
AUSTIN HANSEN
New York, New York

Austin Hansen's career in photography began in the U.S. Virgin Islands, his birthplace. The official Island photographer, Clair Taylor, taught him to handle a camera, and Taylor's son Alvin, Hansen's childhood friend, taught him medical photography. In 1924, the budding photographer took pictures of a hurricane and sold it to the Virgin Islands government for four dollars.

Four years later, Hansen moved to New York where he delivered medicine for a pharmacy in Harlem for five dollars a week and later worked as an elevator operator on Ninth Street when the breadlines and apple-selling in Harlem reflected the suffering of Blacks during the Depression.

His hobby was going to dances and hanging around the drummers who played with the bands in the clubs of Harlem. He bought his first set of drums on the Bowery and had his first gig at Moses Hall in Harlem. In 1930, he studied drumming under the WPA program while studying art and maintaining his elevator operator's job for two years. He had all his gigs at the Rhythm Club, earning three to five dollars a night, and all the bands he played with consisted of Black musicians. Duke of Iron, a musician who influenced Hansen strongly, got him to join the local 802 musicians union of which Hansen is now an honorary member. Playing with the calypso bands, he performed numerous gigs out of town, including the Claridge Hotel, Washington, D.C., where his band had to ask a white person to purchase their sandwiches from a drugstore.

While playing in a Harlem night club, he discovered that a photographer could make more money in an hour than he made in five hours of playing the drums. So he borrowed a Zeiss Ikon from a fellow musician and took pictures in small dance halls. At a tribute to Mrs. Eleanor Roosevelt he took a photo of a Black girl playing the piano which he sold to the *Amsterdam News* for two dollars.

Mr. Baxter Leach, a public relations man, introduced him to various churches such as Mother A.M.E. Zion and St. Martin's where Hansen took pictures regularly of staff and events, and still does so today.

Later his brother, Aubrey, came up from the Virgin Islands to help him and Hansen recalls, "If it weren't for his help, I wouldn't have made it the business it is today."

In World War II, he enlisted in the Navy but was told by a navy mate, "You'll never make it as a photographer in this man's Navy." In Williamsburgh, Virginia, Hansen was sent to the recreation officer who set up a band for him and he "showed them his stuff." Since there was no photographer assigned to his outfit, the construction battalion (Sea Bees), he was sent to California to learn combat/war photography, while still playing with the band. He was given the rank of photographer's mate, 2nd class, an unusual rating for white naval photographers much less for Blacks. In

1945, he worked with the Office of War Information. Since he did not want to transfer to Lake Success, he came back to Harlem to set up the studio that is currently on the same site. This studio is a virtual photo archives, housing photographs of practically every famous Black person, as well as the unknown Black person.

In all the time of his career, Mr. Hansen has helped and trained many young people to get started in photography. Medical photography, protraiture, photojournalism—Austin Hansen has pursued them all. He was a regular photographer for the *Amsterdam News*, the *New York Age*, *African Opinion* and the *People's Voice*. Today he continues his career as photohistorian.

Catering Contractor
LEROY C. TOMBS
Bonner Springs, Kansas

Leroy C. Tombs was born in 1921 in Bonner Springs, Kansas, and remained there until his enlistment in the U.S. Navy in 1938. Among his sea-duty assignments were feeding and housekeeping tasks aboard the USS *Dallas,* the USS *Guardfish* submarine and other submarines, and personnel and recruiting duties for the Navy following World War II.

Upon his retirement from the Navy in 1961, Mr. Tombs became manager of food service and custodial firms in the Kansas City area, the eastern U.S. and the West Coast. His career in the food service industry has been enhanced by community service activities. His feeling for Bonner Springs and his fellow Kansans is measured in part by basing his home office there. He is *ex-officio* ambassador of minorities, the aged and the indigent, and constantly helping those less fortunate than he is.

Maintaining an open-door policy in his private life as well as his business life, Mr. Tombs, as executive director of the local federally financed housing authority, places qualified individuals into low-costing housing. His "self help" philosophy encourages housing recipients to take greater personal interest in the upkeep of themselves, their families and their surroundings.

Mr. Tombs is treasurer of the Bonner Springs Chamber of Commerce. He has served on the Artemus Foundation Board of Trustees, an organization dedicated to assisting high school drop-outs, unwed mothers, juvenile law-breakers and youth with drug-related problems. He also serves on the membership committee of the NAACP.

Mr. Tombs has made his expertise available to several minority-owned businesses in the Kansas City area. He believes that he has the advantage of experience in a field that necessitates a personal commitment to assist other minority and disadvantaged Americans.

The turning point in his career happened in 1971 when he was awarded two Small Business Administration contracts to Fort Riley, Kansas, and Fort Leonard Wood, Missouri. The first contract was obtained on a negotiated rather than on a competitive basis—a first for him. Having spent a lifetime learning and training in the catering field, he felt that he could not develop a market because of insufficient monies, as was frequently the case with minority businesses. The SBA supplied both the market and the funds, and other food service contracts quickly followed. Mr. Tombs became the first Black businessman to participate in the building of the Alaskan pipeline with a subservice contract through Greyhound Support Services.

He was named Kansas Small Businessman of the Year in 1974 and Seller of the Year by the Minority Business Exposition in 1975. He is currently chairman of the nominating committee of the National Association of Service Contractors and is a member of the Kansas Office of Minority Business Enterprise. He also serves on the buyer/seller committee of the Black Economic Union of Kansas City.

Profiles in Black

Leroy Tombs, center, signs multimillion-dollar subcontract with Greyhound Support Services executives.

23

Psychologist
ANNETTE GAINES KEARNEY
Newark, New Jersey

As a very young child Annette Gaines Kearney dreamed of becoming a physician. However, growing up in a society where most professions were closed to Blacks, she was given little encouragement to pursue this ambition. Always a realist, she decided that this dream could be deferred and proceeded to do the next best thing. In deciding to become a teacher, she felt that she could still be of great service to her people.

Her years as an elementary school teacher and guidance counselor in the New Jersey school system proved to be rewarding. She was an inspiring example to many students. Her concern for the welfare of all students stood her in good stead. But the earlier dream of being a doctor never quite left her. In 1968, Dr. Kearney matriculated for a Master's degree in guidance and counseling at Newark State College, New Jersey.

In spite of the demands of her graduate program Dr. Kearney did not allow them to interfere with the private demands of being a wife and mother of two. Unfortunately, as fate would have it, Dr. Kearney became seriously ill. Instead of giving in to the condition, however, Dr. Kearney triumphed and was back into the educational mainstream within months. Looking back, she says, "If I had informed the university of my illness, they would have requested that I withdraw, so from my bed I planned and completed my work with the help of my husband and friends. It was a real personal struggle during those two years and it was all related to my femaleness and blackness—but strong faith, the encouragement of my family, and above all a determination to succeed against all odds, gave me the strength to go on."

From the beginning of her school career Dr. Kearney was not inhibited about being heard or seen. Reticence and silence were not part of Dr. Kearney's makeup. She could not stand to see injustices without protest. An injustice to one, she felt, is an injustice to all.

In 1970, Dr. Kearney obtained her Master's degree and three years later a doctorate in counseling psychiatry from Rutgers University, New Jersey. She succeeded where most men and women would have failed.

At present, Dr. Kearney is assistant executive superintendent in Newark, New Jersey, the largest school system in the state. Although the responsibilities and challenges of this position would be overwhelming for many other people, Dr. Kearney calmly handles each day in its stride. She modestly states, "I only hope that as a Black psychologist, school administrator and, last but certainly not least, a parent, my attempts to instill confidence and community responsibility in children will be meaningful."

Profiles in Black

Restaurant Chain Owner
BRADY KEYS, JR.
Pittsburgh, Pennsylvania

Brady Keys, Jr., born in Austin, Texas, displayed very early an outstanding characteristic that led him into various professions. His only incentive was his self-determination. In 1950, Brady started playing varsity football at Kealing Junior High School in Austin. The next year Brady's family moved to Los Angeles, where he attended Polytechnic High School and became a four-sport sensation, although football was always his first love.

Brady suffered an injury that threatened to cripple him, but a grateful student body raised the money to pay for a knee operation. The doctors' pessimistic predictions of how long it would take before he could walk again—if ever—challenged young Brady's spirit. Eleven days after the operation, he was walking—insisting that he was ready to play football again. His successful recovery deepened Brady's confidence in his ability to overcome any obstacle, and later he did overcome many obstacles. Playing professional ball from 1961-69—six years with the Pittsburgh Steelers and one year each with the Minnesota Vikings and the St. Louis Cardinals—Brady felt that he had accomplished everything in the football profession, when he was named All-Pro. He wanted to fulfill another ambition which was the business world.

He received the same reception when he began business as when he started playing football: People would tell him, "You can't do it!" "You don't have the money to set up a business." Brady remembered how difficult it was playing football, the times when games were tough and he had to keep fighting. And that is exactly how he reacted in his business too.

Today All-Pro Enterprises, Inc., is a profitable business enterprise that focuses on serving fast foods to Black consumers. All-Pro opened with a fried-chicken outlet in San Diego in 1967, and the experience gained at this unit was utilized when the company expanded. Presently All-Pro operates restaurants in Pittsburgh, Pennsylvania; Manhattan, Brooklyn and the Bronx, New York; Cleveland, Ohio; Detroit, Michigan; and has granted franchises to operators of other outlets. All-Pro is listed as the nation's 23rd largest Black-owned business and is ranked as the number one employer of Blacks as listed in the *Black Enterprise's* List of the Top 100 Black Businesses.

Mr. Keys is also the founder and president of Pennky Mining Company, a company involved in the mining and brokering of coal.

Brady Keys attended Colorado State University and majored in business administration. He is presently on the board of directors of the International Franchise Association and is the chairman of the Association's Equal Opportunity Committee. He is also on the President's Council of Carlow College and is a director of the Alumni Association of the Pittsburgh Steelers football club.

Profiles in Black

28

Dramatic Artist
GERTRUDE P. McBROWN
Jamaica, New York

Profiles in Black

Gertrude P. McBrown has made a substantial contribution over the years as author, teacher, historian and dramatic artist. Along with giving lectures, recitals and costumed one-woman shows, she is in constant demand for radio discussions, school assemblies, libraries, churches, college lectures and teacher workshops in African-American history.

While residing in Washington, D.C., she became the founder and director of the District of Columbia Recreation Children's Theatre and the Adult Drama Workshops. Ms. McBrown coordinated the African Folklore and Afro-American dramatizations in the theatre field. She held a long and dedicated association with Dr. Carter G. Woodson, founder of the Association for the Study of Afro-American Life and History and was on the editorial staff of the first bulletins.

When she moved to New York, she taught speech and directed drama groups at the Carnegie Hall Studio.

Ms. Mc Brown initiated the founding of the Carter G. Woodson Memorial Research Collection in the Queens Borough Public Library, Jamaica. Her "Proud Heritage" column that appeared weekly in the *Community Chatter* and other newspapers for several years has taken form in "Proud Heritage" plaques, distributed by Proud Heritage, Inc., of which she is president. She serves the Central Queens community as senior citizen coordinator and youth culture specialist. Her picture poetry book and stories for elementary and high schools are very popular.

Ms. McBrown earned a Bachelor of Arts in drama and literary interpretation from Emerson College in Boston, Massachusetts, and a Master's in education from Boston University. She has studied at the Conservatoire Nationale de Musique et D'Art and took dramatics and advanced literature at the Institut Britannique of the Sorbonne in Paris. She also conducted research in African culture and folklore at the Institute of African Languages and Culture at the Royal Empire Society and the British Museum and the Royal Academy of Dramatic Art in London. She has traveled extensively in Africa, studying in Senegal and the Institute of African Studies in Ibadan, Nigeria, where she performed in storytelling and dance groups.

Listed among her awards are citations from the St. Albans Civic Improvement Association, National Association of Negro Business and Professional Women's Club, National Conference of Christians and Jews, the Association for the Preservation and Presentation of Cultural Arts, Urban League, Omega Psi Phi fraternity and Phi Delta Kappa sorority.

Ms. McBrown is a member of the Executive Council Association for the Study of Afro-American Life and History and delegate to the United Nations.

Pilot, Weathercaster
JAMES ALPHONSO TILMON, SR.
Highland Park, Illinois

When he was eight years old, James Tilmon saw a plane in the sky and knew he wanted to be a pilot. His father, a high school principal, gave young James and his brother a good education. James Tilmon, born in Guthrie, Oklahoma, received his early education in his native state. He went on to Howard University, intending to take premedical courses, but two years later switched to music at Tennessee A & I State University in Nashville. He attended Maryland State College, Princess Anne, Maryland, for one semester, and finished his studies in music at Lincoln University, Jefferson City, Missouri.

Before graduation, Tilmon realized that there were no Black clarinetists in any major orchestras. The only choice left was teaching. But his interest in aviation remain unabated. He joined the ROTC at Tennessee State, where a white military science professor wrote on Tilmon's record that he lacked aptitude for aviation. However, Tilmon was saved from this damaging but groundless write-up when a Black military science professor at Lincoln permitted him to take engineering courses, even though he missed the first semester. He graduated with top grades.

Afterward, he served eight years with the Army Corps of Engineers. At Fort Leonard Wood, Missouri, he recalls, "I was one of two Blacks applying for flight school, although there was a lack of interest and a shortage of officers. I was surprised to be accepted." He was transferred to San Marcos, Texas, for primary aviation training, then on to Fort Rucker, Alabama, for advanced flight training in 1959. "About six Black students forewarned me that only one or two from each class would make it, and although I couldn't accept this racism, I couldn't do anything about it. The other guy washed out." At a graduation party an instructor shocked Tilmon by pronouncing, "You people (meaning Blacks) are all alike—either really great or not worth a damn."

During instrument flight training in Alabama, trainee pilots landed in civilian fields. Tilmon went hungry many times when he was refused service at segregated restaurants. He preserved his self-image by thinking of himself as an officer first without regard to race.

In 1961, he studied at a helicopter school in Mineral Wells, Texas. The next year he was assigned to Germany, where the white commanding officer requested Tilmon's transfer, but he stayed on staff—in name only. Col. John C.H. Lee, Jr., became his new commanding officer and gave him the responsibility and respect he merited. Although Tilmon won an Army commendation medal and worked hard, on later assignments he was frequently given duties below his rank because he was Black.

In 1965, American Airlines heard of Tilmon's flying abilities and offered him a job. He was the third Black pilot to be hired by American. He expects to be a full-fledged captain by November 1976.

Profiles in Black

Wanting to be more productive in his spare time, he was invited to host a program "Our People," on public service television in Chicago. Though challenging, the job was not lucrative, so he formed his own Tilmon Productions company in 1970. "Tilmon Tempos," his weekly program went to NBC and won an Emmy award. In the fall of 1974, he became a TV weathercaster five nights a week on NBC. Mr. Tilmon has founded a second company, Tilmon Enterprises, a consulting firm.

He has received numerous awards: (Chicago) West Side Organization, No. 1 Award, 1975; the Black Achievers Award, YMCA: the Captain's Chair Award, from American Airlines, 1969, among others. He serves on the board of various music-affiliated and educational associations.

Only when I myself became a teen-ager did the dream of America begin to taste sour in my mouth. I was not a good student, nor was I a bad one. Then followed a teen-age period of being in school for a time and then out of it to help out. I was the firstborn of four. At a time when the white boys I knew were still going to school, I was riding the sanitation-department trucks and tossing up steel barrels filled with ashes. Even some of my black friends had not had to leave school. I spent my evenings dripping bitterness and trying to take extra classes at night to catch up.

—John A. Williams

Author (<u>Night Song, The Angry Ones, Sissie, The Man Who Cried I Am</u>, others)

Ethnomusicologist
ESI SYLVIA KINNEY
New York, New York

Ethnomusicology, according to Webster's definition, is the study of the music of non-European cultures. Esi Sylvia Kinney's decision to enter the field of ethnomusicology, and also the field of choreography, was a result of her early childhood ambition to become a jazz pianist and dancer, and as a reaction to "an abusive school system's effort to instill inferiority in Black students." She learned to counteract the abuses by clinging to the Black community and her family, who had always imbued in her a high regard for herself and Black people. In fact, she never felt inferior until she encountered racism at school.

The institutionalized racism did not have any effect on her development but it did provoke a strong urge in her to probe what she describes as "the basis of our ethnicity and our role in society." She admits to having resorted to subterfuge in her research, dissection and analysis of the conflicting and erroneous material she received in school because "to openly contest damaging principles or imposed values was to invite greater disaster."

In 1960, Ms. Kinney wrote her Master's thesis on African music although "there were no other Africanists around to help—or hinder—me." That body of analyses gave her the tools to travel to Latin America and to conduct research in several dynamic Black societies. She went to live in Ghana in 1965 to research the cultures of the Ashanti and Dagomba peoples. The period in Africa afforded her the opportunity to travel extensively throughout the continent and to perform and write numerous articles based on her research.

Since her return to the United States, she has been waging a campaign to present Africans in the proper perspective. She is continuing her independent research on the relationship of Afro-American culture to that of the Motherland. She is currently writing a book on the ritual foundation of Black performing arts in the Americas.

Assistant Principal
THEODORE JOSIAH HAIG
Providence, Rhode Island

Theodore Josiah Haig was born in the Bronx, New York, one of nine children and received his primary education in New York and his secondary education at James Monroe High School. He says, "Like many young Black males growing up in an urban area like New York, I found the basketball court was the only place I could seek refuge from facing the frustrating realities in our complex society."

During his high school years he realized the significance of an education in helping him cope with those "realities" and, although he was not a high achiever academically, he was sincere, dedicated and extremely motivated. His high school basketball coach was the supportive adult in young Theodore's life, and aided him in obtaining an athletic scholarship to Nathaniel Hawthorne College in Antrim, New Hampshire. The young scholar worked through his first year with academic honors.

However, the childhood dream of playing basketball in Madison Square Garden in New York induced him to transfer to Providence College in Rhode Island where athletes on scholarship were more visible to pro basketball teams and he finished there in 1970 with a Bachelor of Arts degree and later obtained his Master's degree in educational administration and supervision from Rhode Island College in 1973. He is currently working on his doctoral thesis and due to receive his Ph.D. from Boston College. While working on his doctorate he was appointed assistant principal for instructor in a desegregated high school in Providence. Theodore Haig still has a career aspiration—to be a superintendent of schools in an urban district.

He is married to the former Lynda Blunt and they have one daughter, Diane. He asserts that the marriage was "the turning point" in his career and his life because of the strong and mature atmosphere created from their marriage and the atmosphere helped him to become more analytical and conscientious about potentials in himself. Apparently, other people concur, for Theodore Haig is highly regarded by his peers, by his supervisors who give him the highest commendations in regard to his work and, the many young people whom he counsels and to whom he gives so much in time and high-level energy.

Profiles in Black

38

Record Producer
TASHA THOMAS
New York, New York

Although Tasha Thomas considers herself a bona fide New Yorker, the major part of her life was spent in Jeuntyn, Alaska, where her parents were working for the federal government. Tasha had only minimal contact with the other Black families who, like her own, were temporarily stationed in Jeuntyn.

She remembers as a child that she was pretty much isolated, but by singing gospel in church, she developed a strong ambition to sing professionally and eventually to get out into the world.

In 1968, the venturous Tasha landed in New York City. She admits to experiencing a mild case of "culture shock" due to the fast pace of city life. But she quickly adjusted herself to the reality of her situation and searched for employment. In two years she held approximately 40 jobs, from secretarial to whatever, deciding to "do bad until things got better."

Things improved only after Tasha acknowledged the saying "It's not what you know, but who you know." She quickly began to make contact with people in the recording industry to get her own profession moving. Her first recording session took place in 1969 at a major record company where she sang backup for prominent artists. At that time she met Carl Hall, who was also singing background. The two of them decided to go into business for themselves and formed Thomas-Hall Productions.

Their company produces and performs its own commercials for radio and television. Some of the company's most important clients have been Yago Sangria, Pepsi Cola, Mountain Dew and Country Club Malt liquor. Thomas-Hall Productions also composes and performs backgrounds for many leading artists in the jazz, rock and blues fields. Some of the artists it has backed are Esther Phillips, James Brown, Stevie Wonder and Lena Horne.

Tasha Thomas attributes her success to an ability to know exactly what she wants and how to go after it. She feels that being a woman makes it easier for her to maneuver in business circles because the entertainment business is dominated by males. Tasha believes men will acquiesce more easily to ideas and suggestions of a woman than those of another man. Whether or not men are being condescending does not bother Tasha: she is concerned with getting over—and she does.

Tasha has not formed an opinion as to whether or not being Black in her position has any particular advantages or disadvantages. However, she has encountered certain Black performers who have been particularly "vicious" toward her. In general, though, she feels she is respected by

Profiles in Black

others in her field—both Black and white—and, as president of Thomas-Hall Productions, she feels she is a success.

Her advice to those who want to break into the recording business is to not jump in right away but to learn to listen, musically or business-wise. Ms. Thomas hopes to open a "clinic" that will help the young gospel singers "sitting on the church steps" to learn the professional aspects of singing and recording.

Police Officer
EDDIE J. ANDERSON
Brooklyn, New York

Eddie J. Anderson, born in Brooklyn, New York, recalls of his past, "Although I was a product of the public school system, I received a substantial amount of education from two other sources: my parents and the Streets. The Streets taught me that discrimination exists, that frustration prevails, that crime and drugs are ever present. My parents have taught me something I have cherished—self-esteem and confidence in myself." His parents' counsel was profound and long lasting—armaments to effectively fight off the influence of the Street, to think and act as an individual and not be influenced by the wishes and utterances of others.

Eddie Anderson joined the New York City Police Department in 1966 at a time when there was a low percentage of Blacks on the force because the civil service examination was geared to prevent many Blacks from passing due to the socio-economic condition of the period and the negative attitude Blacks had toward the police. The department has sought to change these conditions and attitudes, and Anderson thinks they have made some progress through a variety of programs that includes community councils, dialogue programs and, through the media, the education of the public to operations of the police department. Anderson feels there has been improved cooperation of the public and police to rid crime in the streets. Because of the improved image, there has been an increase of new Black police officers, both male and female. Courses are available in career orientation, management or college credits.

Eddie Anderson began his own police career at the 32nd Precinct in Harlem with the narcotics division, and is currently a member of the youth gang task force in Jamaica, New York. He says of his work, "These assignments have given me a feeling of self-satisfaction and achievement, knowing that in my way I have helped to solve the problems of those with whom I have been in contact and, while doing so, hopefully, I have changed the image of the police officer."

He deals with youths on a one-to-one basis. Anderson thinks that one of the roots of youthful crime is the lack of individualism because peer group pressure is so great and that drop-outs from school could and do become easily involved with the law. One of his methods of dealing with the problem, he says, is, "When I confront these people I try to impress upon them the ideals of first being an individual—to take pride in yourself—and second to be confident that you can achieve your goals. I tell them that there are many fields of endeavor open to Blacks that have been closed in the past, but they require a good education and fortitude. Quality education should not be scoffed at or taken lightly. The doors to success are ajar; one push and they'll be wide open. The opportunities are limitless for those who believe in themselves, are willing to work hard and have the confidence that if they apply themselves they can succeed."

Profiles in Black

Concert/Opera Singer
CLAUDIA LINDSEY
New York, New York

Claudia Lindsey was born in Harlem at home. Her father, a struggling young minister from Mississippi, was a fine example of dedication as he attended night school and often brought young Claudia with him. Her childhood was filled with the usual activities of any Black child—living, playing and fighting in the Streets. "But," she recalls, "the reality of the Street meant maintaining a mental and physical readiness to ward off the danger of ghetto living."

In public school, frustrated by the lack of challenge to her abilities, Claudia found herself becoming a problem. Her parents had her "bused" to a racially mixed school where she was salutatorian of her class. Later she attended Brandeis University, Waltham, Massachusetts, as one of 12 Black students in an enrollment of 1,000. She majored in political science with the idea of continuing in law. The strong pull that she felt toward music she denied in herself because she had seen so many talented Black musicians fall tragically by the wayside. However, her musical talents could not go unheeded forever, and after finishing college she returned to New York City "determined to pursue this course regardless..."

Supporting herself with work in a publishing house, she, like her father before her, studied at night. She recalls, "It took many years and a great deal of persistence. I auditioned and finally succeeded in securing a job as soloist with the Little Orchestra Society." Of her appearance, Harold Schoenberg of the *New York Times* wrote, "Outstanding was the soprano Claudia Lindsey, opulent of voice and secure in style. This young woman has everything on her side."

She toured the United States and Canada as a solo recitalist. Her operatic debut was as Clara in the New York City Opera production of "Porgy and Bess." She appeared as Bess to Cab Calloway's Sporting Life with the Atlanta and National symphonies. Touring with both the Metropolitan Opera National Company and the Western Opera Theater of San Francisco, she has sung leading roles in "The Marriage of Figaro," "The Rape of Lucretia," "La Boheme" and "Cosi fan tutte."

"Nothing came easily," she states. "I have no proof that certain refusals of work were due to my being Black. People certainly won't admit that they are not engaging you because you're Black. The struggle to overcome obstacles persists all of one's life. A carefully preserved sense of 'self-worth' and a 'fighting spirit' have been great sustaining forces in my life."

A major breakthrough in her career occurred in 1970 when she starred in the American premiere of Frederick Delius's opera "Koanga," produced by the Opera Society of Washington (D.C.). Her performance was so well received that she recreated her role of Palmyra in the Camden Festival production in London and recorded the opera on Angel Records. Paul Hume of the *Washington Post* wrote "Claudia Lindsey's Palmyra is a jewel."

She has sung with many major orchestras such as the Atlanta, Dallas, Milwaukee and National symphonies in the U.S. and the London Symphony abroad. From 1970-73, Ms. Lindsey served as an Affiliate Artist at LeMoyne-Owen College in Memphis, Tennessee. She has appeared on WNET-TV and on the "Today Show." She is the recipient of numerous awards and fellowships, including the Metropolitan Opera Stoughton Award. *Opera News* has called her "a soprano with authentic star quality."

44

Magazine Publisher
EDWARD LEWIS
New York, New York

Edward Lewis began his work career at Citibank of New York where he was a "budding banker" until he attended a conference sponsored by a large Wall street brokerage firm on how to attract more Blacks into establishing more Black businesses. At the synposium it was suggested that there might be a market for a fashion magazine for Black women. Those interested in the project grouped together, including Edward Lewis, who resigned his bank job in May 1969 to guide the "money problems" of *Essence* Magazine.

Financing for *Essence* proved difficult. On both Wall Street and Madison Avenue, Lewis encountered resistance. He recalls, "The skepticism that investors and advertisers showed was both of a professional and a racial nature. Several things operated against us: we were without publishing experience and opening a new magazine, while other publishers were closing their doors and—we were black. Our debut issue that came out a year later sold 75,000 of the 200,000 copies printed; it lacked editorial focus. It was too stylized, too intellectual and irrelevant to all but maybe one per cent of Black women and that one per cent was reading *Vogue* or *Harper's Bazaar*."

Playboy, Inc. took over *Essence* in June 1970 with a sizable investment. In 1971, Lewis was named publisher.

Prior to entering the business world, Lewis attended the University of New Mexico where he earned his Master's degree in political science with a minor in international relations. He played on the University's football team and thought about a career in pro ball until "I was unceremoniously cut from the team because I was at best—mediocre." At DeWitt Clinton High School in his native Bronx, New York, he had excelled in both the guard and full back positions and was named "All City" in 1957, earning the Lou Gehrig Award for courage and sportsmanship. Lewis recounts, "Being cut from the squad at New Mexico opened my eyes to the harsher realities of life and initially I thought to enter politics and/or business. I felt if the system was to be changed—at the very least made responsible to Blacks—it could only be done through the political system or through money. Black money is Black business." Lewis returned to New York where he is working on a doctorate in public administration at New York University.

A bachelor, Lewis is a firm believer in "a heightened awareness for Blacks in what it means to be Black. Black power means more input into the economic system. It means pride—*self* pride," he continues. And although more Blacks than ever before are gaining it, more self-esteem is needed. More Blacks are at the center of political power fighting for economic opportunities for minorities. But they are still faced with

Profiles in Black

the same trilogy of demands in this country; unavailable jobs, housing and education. Through *Essence* we fight for greater self awareness, greater Black pride, which we believe will result in more and more Black people demanding that their rights and demands be considered in all branches of government and power."

Government Administrator
BENJAMIN LACY HUNTON
Arlington, Virginia

Benjamin Lacy Hunton began his career in 1942, teaching in junior and senior high schools in Washington, D.C. In 1951, he was promoted to supervising director of the school system, a post he held for seven years. He became part of the superintendent staff in 1958, and eight years later left the school system to become an area director with the Equal Education Opportunity Program, a division of the Department of Health, Education and Welfare. In 1969, he was coordinator of the Job Corps Program Support Staff with the Department of the Interior in Washington, D.C. The following year he became assistant administrator of the Education and Training, Mining Enforcement and Safety Administration, also part of the Department of the Interior, a position he presently holds.

Dr. Hunton's second career was in the military. He attended the U.S. Army Command and General Staff College, Fort Leavenworth, Kansas, in 1952; the Industrial College of the Armed Forces in 1958; the Armored School where he took a course in Senior Officer Preventive Maintenance in 1961; The Ordnance School, where he learned about guided missiles and nuclear weapons in 1962; a chemical, biological and radiological (CBR) weapon orientation course in 1967; and the Army War College, Carlisle, Pennsylvania, in 1971. He served seven years in World War II with the army as a second lieutenant and became colonel, commanding the 1st Brigade, 80th Division. He was promoted to Brigadier General, Office of the Chief of Reserve Components, in 1971, and was promoted to Major General and assigned to the 97th ARCOM, Fort Meade, Maryland, in 1972. He has been an officer of the Reserves since 1949. Dr. Hunton has been awarded a Meritorious Service Medal, World War II Victory Medal, American Theatre Service Medal and Armed Forces Reserve Medal with Hour Glass.

Dr. Hunton is also the author of two publications about the school system, "Study of Selected School Dropouts, 1963-1966" and "Basic Track in Junior High Schools," along with several magazine articles. He is a member of the Kentucky Mining Institute; Interior Liaison—The White House Committee on Civil Rights and Minority Affairs; AMVETS; and the Washington Urban League, among others. In 1975, he was recipient of the Howard University Distinguished Alumni Award.

Dr. Hunton was born in Washington, D.C., in 1919. He obtained his Bachelor and Master of Arts degrees at Howard University in 1940 and 1942, respectively, and a doctorate in public administration from American University in 1954. Dr. Hunton and his wife Jean have one son, Benjamin.

Profiles in Black

Legal Counsel
BARBARA SCOTT PREISKEL
New York, New York

Barbara Scott Preiskel's unusual career as vice president and legislative counsel for the Motion Picture Association and as a director of Amstar Corporation, Jewel Companies, and Textron began with her education at two institutions open to Blacks. She recalls, "Being able to get a good educational background at Wellesley College and Yale University back in the days when quotas for Blacks and women were still very much to be reckoned with must be considered a major force in my career."

She obtained her Bachelor of Arts degree at Wellesley, Massachusetts (1945), and her Bachelor of Laws degree at Yale, New Haven, Connecticut (1947). She was admitted to the Bar Associations of Washington, D.C., and New York a year later and was appointed law clerk to the Hon. Charles E. Wyzanski of the U.S. District Court, Boston, Massachusetts.

In 1949, she gained a position with a Wall Street firm and was later an associate with two law firms before moving on to the Motion Picture Association. She has developed the MPA's legislative department into an important part of the Association.

While pursuing her career, Ms. Preiskel has devoted much time to civic and extracurricular affairs, such as chairmanship of the board of the Wiltwyck School for Boys, which serves New York City boys, and with the American Civil Liberties Union and the Federation of Protestant Welfare Agencies.

She has also served on the executive committee and the committees on family court and family law, sex and the law, judiciary, etc., of the Bar Association of the City of New York. She was a member of the President's Commission on Obscenity and Pornography from 1968-70. While working many hours with these committees, she came into contact with civic and business leaders in the community. Because her reputation as a distinguished lawyer and Association officer became known to public corporations who, in the late Sixties, were seeking a broader representation of minorities and women for their boards, Ms. Preiskel was invited to serve on several corporate boards.

Barbara Scott Preiskel is married to an attorney, Robert H. Preiskel, and they have two sons.

Profiles in Black

Law Professor
JEROME SHUMAN
Washington, D.C.

Jerome Shuman, Professor of Law at Georgetown University Law Center, was born in 1937 in St. Augustine, Florida. Mr. Shuman's father, Will, was a construction laborer and did migratory farm work along with his family. They moved to New Jersey when Jerome was 12. When he was attending high school, he was asked twice to leave, once for academic failure and the second time for fighting with a classmate. But his spirit remained undaunted and he graduated from Richard J. Murray High School in his native city.

Profiles in Black

If young Jerome had followed in the paths of those around him, he never would have gone to college; however, Jerome was of a different mind. He wanted to become a lawyer and was determined to attain his goal. He persuaded the dean of Trenton Junior College to allow him to enroll without any entrance exam, applications or transcripts. When his rather undistinguished high school record arrived, however, his academic performance had been so good at Trenton that any notion to ask him to leave was promptly dispelled.

Jerome Shuman went to Howard University in Washington, D.C., earning in 1960 a Bachelor of Arts degree in political science and a minor in accounting. In further pursuit of education he graduated *cum laude* with a Bachelor of Law degree from Howard and the next year a Master's from Yale University. He worked his way through school by taking odd jobs.

At Howard, Jerome Shuman was appointed a research assistant and the Notes Editor for the Howard Law Journal. He was the Regional Winner of the American Law Student Association's opinion letter-writing contest. He won an award for outstanding debate and the senior class achievement award. Later he obtained a Sterling Fellowship at Yale Law School.

Mr. Shuman has taught in the law schools of Georgetown, Howard, Rutgers, Tennessee, Cincinnati and the American universities. He also has worked with the Federal Trade Commission and has served as consultant to the Department of Health, Education and Welfare and to the Administration Conference of the U.S. He was the first director of the Office of Equal Opportunity at the Department of Agriculture. He has been the secretary of the Council of Black Appointees and has held membership on the boards of directors with the National Consumer Information Center, the Upward Mobility Board and the District of Columbia chapter of the Federal Bar Association.

Mr. Shuman is listed in *Who's Who in the South and Southeast*. He received the outstanding professor award at Howard Law School. He was given the key to the city and made an honorary citizen of Baton Rouge, Louisiana, in 1973.

He has written articles and given many speeches such as "Creating Your Own Opportunities," "Opportunities for Black Lawyers," "The Responsibility of the Modern Corporations to Society" and "Anti-trust Problems Involved in Franchising Selling."

Education Administrator
FREDDIE LANG GROOMES
Tallahassee, Florida

Dr. Freddie Lang Groomes has spent several years counseling students and working with parents and community organizations. She says, "I am committed to improving the circumstances of people, particularly Black people and women by assisting them through education and employment to obtain an improved quality of life regardless of their socioeconomic background, their race or their sex."

As she worked through her counseling career, however, she realized that there was a need for being an educator as well "for those persons who are pursuing training or additional expertise in support service."

But further, Dr. Groomes felt the need to "be actively involved in policy formation and the administrative aspects of programs that indeed influence young people relating to education."

Therefore, Dr. Groomes took on the job of providing leadership in the writing and development of a pilot program in the state university system. The affirmative action program was designed to aid minorities and women in the work force at Florida State University as well as in general employment and higher education.

Dr. Freddie Lang Groomes was born in Jacksonville, Florida. She earned her Bachelor's degree in home economics and her Master's in guidance and counseling, both from Florida A & M University. She received her Doctor of Philosophy degree in counseling education (Counseling and Human Systems) at Florida University.

Dr. Groomes was appointed in November 1975 by Gov. Reubin O'D. Askew to chair the Florida Governor's Commission on the Status of Women. She is a member of the Governor's Commission on Indian Affairs, a member of the Florida Human Relations Commission and of the Southern Regional Council. She also serves as consultant to the Department of Health, Education and Welfare, Washington, D.C.

"I have committed my services in the past and will continue to work toward the development and enhancement of Black people, young and old, and poor people to ensure that they are given equal opportunity, experience equity as it relates to education and employment, and to assist in development of skills and the removal of discriminating barriers. I shall continue to work within the system to get more persons active in service and employment, education and research, especially as it relates to improving circumstances and responses to members of oppressed groups."

Profiles in Black

Dr. Freddie Lang Groomes speaks with First Lady, Mrs. Betty Ford. President Gerald Ford is in background.

The man who contents himself to sit down and exemplify the virtue of patience and endurance will find no sympathy from the busy, restless crowd that rush by him. Even the "sick man" must get out of the way when he hears the tramp of the approaching host, or be crushed by the heedless and massive car of progress. Blind Bartimeuses are silenced by the crowd. The world requires active service; it respects only productive workers. The days of hermits and monks have passed away. Action—work, work—is the order of the day. Heroes in the strife and struggle of humanity are the demand of the age. (1862)

—Edward W. Blyden

Educator, Missionary, Black Freedom Activist

Jazz Musician
CHARLES WALTER RAINEY III
Los Angeles, California

Charles Walter Rainey, III, son of Eloise and Charles W. Rainey, Jr., was born in Cleveland, Ohio. He, his sister and parents moved to Youngstown, Ohio, when Chuck was seven. At school he studied the violin and at home basic piano and music theory. Listening to his parents play, he would later pick out chords, whether from Beethoven's work or pop and gospel tunes. He especially liked his father's version of Fats Waller arrangements.

His uncle gave him a trumpet when he was 12, and within an hour of receiving it, the young experimenting musician was producing clear tones. His mother enrolled him with Howard Ramsey at the Strouss-Hirshberg Music Center.

Two years later found him playing with the Farrell (Pennsylvania) Elks Marching Band. He also played with the Trojan Military Band of Youngstown, the only self-supporting, all-Black marching band in the area.

He took up other brass instruments in high school under the tutelage of John Busch, the teacher who influenced him most and with whom he studied the longest. After school and on weekends he sang with a quartet and played trumpet with a trio.

Upon graduation from high school, Chuck Rainey put in six months in the Army Reserves, singing in a quartet and in a duet with his bunk mate. Afterward Rainey received a scholarship from the United Negro College Fund and attended Lane College, Jackson Tennessee, where he played baritone horn with the Brass Ensemble and continued developing in music. After college he returned to Youngstown and played with local rhythm and blues groups.

In Cleveland, Rainey worked with Syl Austin, among other artists. Later he landed a job with the California Playboy in New York City. For several years, he worked with many prominent artists such as King Curtis, Sam Cooke and Etta James, touring the U.S. and Europe. In 1971, he moved from New York to Los Angeles, where he concentrated on recording. His bass work can be heard in themes for popular television serials, radio and TV commercials, movies and shows.

Composer, arranger and producer, Chuck Rainey is also instructor and writer. He teaches bass with the Dick Grove Workshops. He has written a book *Discipline of Emotion,* a study of the electric bass, and he also writes a monthly column, "Chuck Rainey's Modern Bass Guitar," for *Guitar Player Magazine.* He serves on the Judge's Committee at Notre Dame University's Collegiate Jazz Festival.

He is married to Joyce Stroud, a communications graduate of San Francisco State University.

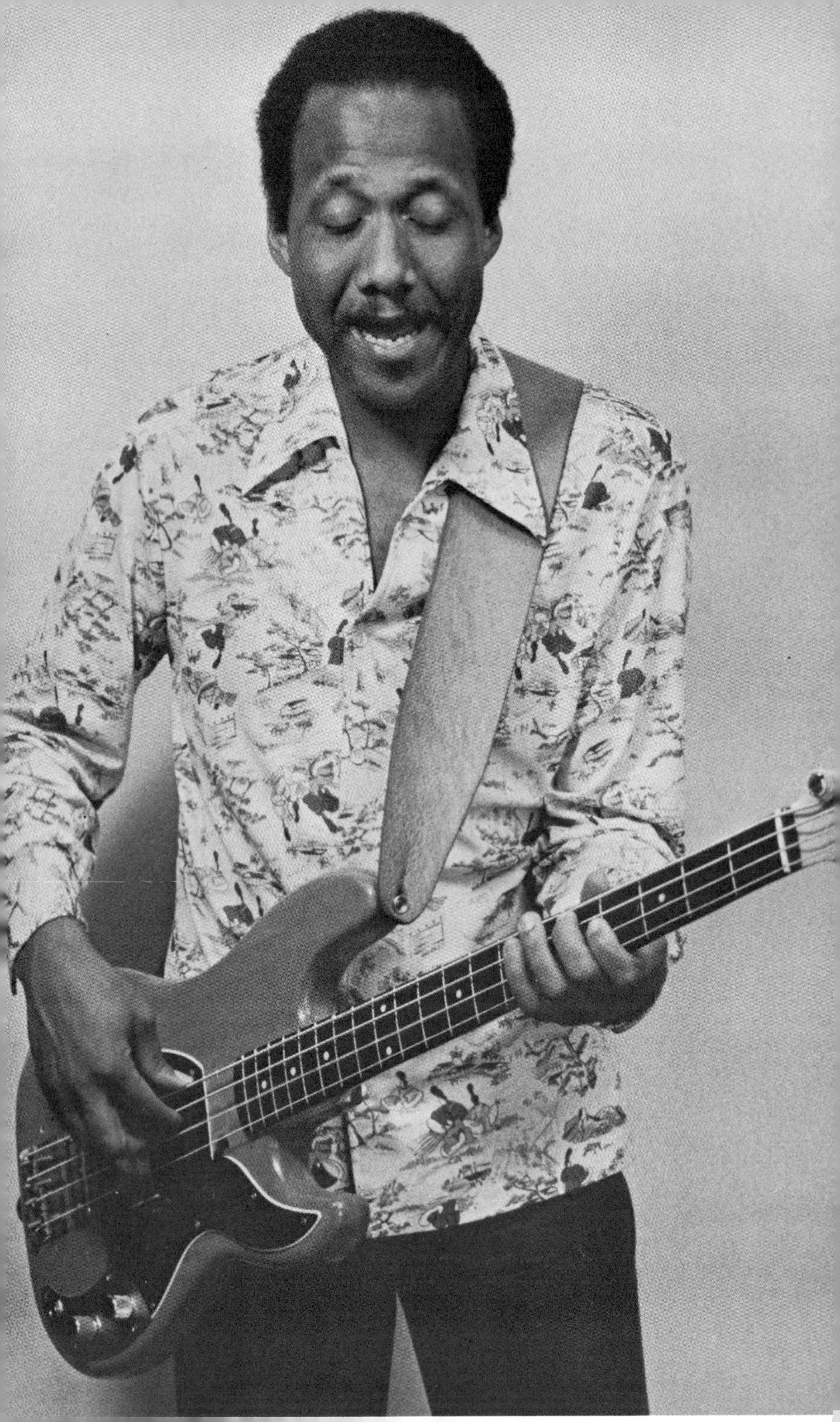

Certified Public Accountant
LARZETTE GOLDEN HALE
Logan, Utah

Larzette Golden Hale was born in 1920 on a share-cropping farm in Idabel, Oklahoma. When their father died, 11-year-old Larzette and her sister, Essie, were sent to an orphanage in Taft, Oklahoma, because their mother couldn't care for them during the Depression. They graduated from high school in 1936 with Larzette the valedictorian of her class.

"At the orphanage I worked under Mrs. Brooks and Mrs. Mason, two fine bookkeepers; from them I developed the desire to become a çertified public account," Prof. Hale recalls. Her mother got a job later at the State Mental Hospital for Negroes near the orphanage, working a 12-hour day for less than $50 per month. From both their earnings, Mrs. Golden's daughters were able to attend Langston University in Oklahoma.

Larzette Golden met William Henri Hale in their freshman year at Langston University and they married after graduation. A *summa cum laude* graduate, she was employed as a secretary while he studied for his Master's. She later obtained her own Master's in accounting in 1943 from Langston. They joined the staff at Bethune-Cookman College, Daytona Beach, Florida, she as secretary to the president and instructor in accounting. She was professor of accounting and chairman of the business administration department working directly with Mrs. Mary McCloud Bethune in the development of the National Council of Negro Women.

In the fall of 1948, Prof. Hale and her husband joined the faculty of Clarke College, Atlanta, Georgia. She received her doctorate in accounting and finance from the University of Wisconsin, passed the CPA examination and opened her own office in 1955. "I was the first Black woman to pass the CPA and earn a doctorate. I served as chairman of the business administration department."

When her husband became president of Langston University in 1960, they led the plans for the physical and educational development and fundraising for faculty and staff. After she closed her office in 1964, she served as director of development. Her husband is now deceased.

In 1966, Prof. Hale was the national president of Alpha Kappa Alpha Sorority, in which position she initiated many programs. She is currently engaged in two research projects and is teaching the theory of accounting. She also teaches intermediate accounting and auditing.

Prof. Hale is a member of the trustee board of the Presbyterian Church of Logan and is the present chairman, the Logan AAUW chapter and Logan Business and Professional Women's chapter. She is a member of the American Accounting Association, the National Association of Black Accountants and is a member of the board of the American Woman's Society of Certified Public Accountants.

Profiles in Black

Journeyman Air Traffic Controller
ALONZA CUMMINGS
Brooklyn, New York

Alonza Cummings, a native of Beaufort, South Carolina, was about seven months old when his mother died at age 18. He was raised by his grandparents. After graduating from high school in 1962, he served in the Air Force for four years. During his tour of duty he was a ground-equipment mechanic. He worked as a warehouseman in the supply department of the Philadelphia Navy Yard. When there was a heavy layoff of workers at the Navy Yard, he attended school to learn air conditioning and refrigeration work. The guidance counselor at the school informed him about work in air traffic control. After taking a government test in 1970 and passing it, he was offered a job at a government service rating of 7, which he turned down. The reason he gives is: "I would have had to go down to the FAA (Federal Aviation Administration) Academy for twelve weeks and since I had no experience in air traffic control, I know that I would not have made it, so I wrote the FAA to consider me at some future date."

The following year, he was offered another controller's job at a lower GS rating at John F. Kennedy Airport. He says, "This time I accepted because I would be attending school for six months with fellows who like myself didn't have the background either. At least I would have a fair chance to learn."

Working as a GS12 journeyman at JFK Airport in Jamaica, New York, Alonza Cummings loves and enjoys what he considers not an ordinary job. He says, "As far as prejudice goes, as long as one is Black—and if I were to be born again, I wouldn't want to be anything else—a person will always run into it. Of course, there is prejudice in the FAA; I was told that I would never make it as a controller because I talked too fast and had an accent. I felt that this was not my fault—how did they expect somebody from South Carolina to sound in New York? Prejudice is something I learned to deal with a long time ago. When they tell me that they don't think I can do something and I know that they're only saying it because I'm Black—well, that makes me try harder to show them that I can."

With approximately 15,000 air traffic controllers in the U.S., Mr. Cummings finds this profession carries a lot of respect and responsibility that "places a lot of people's lives in our hands everyday."

He advises, "As for a person just starting out in life and doesn't know what to do but has what it takes, I would recommend the field of air traffic control."

Profiles in Black

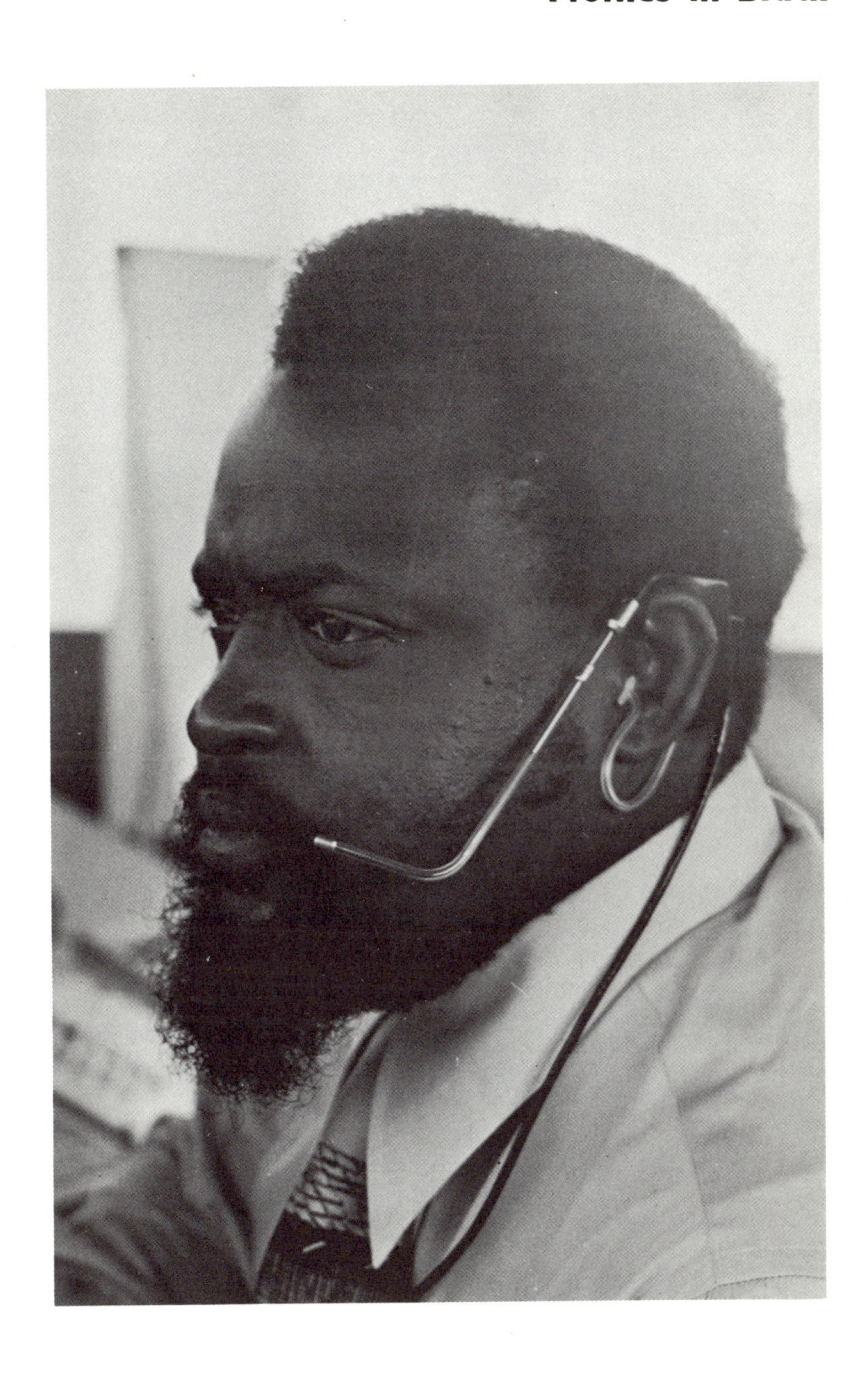

Religious Garment Manufacturer
HENRI O'BRYANT
Los Angeles, California

Henri O'Bryant, Jr., was born in Abberville, Louisiana, in 1908— a time close enough to slavery for him to know it existed but enough in the past for him to see that a better life was possible. "We weren't too far from slavery then," he says. "In some parts of the country they were still carrying it on."

O'Bryant's family—his father Henri, Sr., and mother Virginia and their nine children—were poor sharecroppers who tried to eke out a living by growing sugar cane, watermelons, potatoes, corn and cotton. When young Henri wasn't helping with the farm chores, he assisted his mother who took in sewing to help ends meet. Later the family moved to Lafayette, where O'Bryant attended school for the first time. "Back in those days you didn't go to school by age. You went by size. But by the time I was nine, I was big enough. I went to school consistently after that. I never did miss."

Later the family moved to New Orleans where Henri O'Bryant entered J.W. Hoffman Elementary School and completed the eighth grade. Afterward he attended Xavier Preparatory School, Morris Brown, Atlanta, Georgia, where the high school and college were combined, graduating at age 21; and later returned to New Orleans where he graduated from the University's Gilbert Academy. However, he has bitter memories of fighting for his education:

"The family wanted me to go to work, but I wanted to go to school. This particular day I had been sewing all day. I left a note in the sewing-machine drawer. I knew my mother wouldn't sew on Sunday and I had an extra day before they realized that I had run away."

Arriving at Morris Brown penniless in the dead of winter, the dauntless Henri persuaded the registrar to let him shovel snow and do other odd jobs for his tuition. He made spending money by delivering papers and altering clothes for students and professors.

He received a Julius Rosenwald Foundation scholarship to study YMCA administration at George Williams College in Chicago. He recalls the college years fondly "because I was brought right out of the South and placed on a campus with white and Black students which was a new experience for me."

While he was attending college he got married. Even though he worked for the famous Wabash "Y" he was always plying his tailoring trade. After graduation he worked for the Urban League in Chicago for one year at $9.50 a week.

Later he took a job as a valet, pressing clothes at the Palmolive Building, where he got to know most of the advertising executives. "I used to go around and shine their shoes and press their suits." When O'Bryant's

Profiles in Black

boss decided to leave, the building management installed an elite haberdashery and valet service which O'Bryant managed until the war began. "When World War II started, I couldn't buy any supplies and clothing. The war squeezed me out of business."

He worked at odd jobs for six months including work on a farm in Tucson, Arizona, and entered the Navy in 1942 where he became a physical education instructor.

Henri O'Bryant, now based in Los Angeles, has become one of America's successful religious garment manufacturers. The silver-haired former pants presser owns manufacturing outlets in Hollywood, Oakland, Cleveland, New Orleans, Nashville, Atlanta, Detroit, Raleigh and Charlotte with plans for a dozen more. Late in 1975, he unveiled his Program for Economic Growth (PEG) in Nashville, Tennessee. This program, which teaches Blacks how to upgrade their businesses, has been adopted in Los Angeles and other cities. PEG stimulates Black churches and other organizations to purchase goods and services from Black businesses, thus helping to keep the Black economy flowing.

Theologian
JACQUELYN GRANT
New York, New York

Reverend Jacquelyn Grant holds strong opinions about women in the ministry. "More Black women ministers are needed. Furthermore, Black women are needed in the field of systematic theology. There are no Black women with doctorates in systematic theology and I hope to be the first, but I also hope that others will enter the field. I see as a part of my God-given responsibility to serve as an inspiration to women who are thinking about and seeking to enter the ministry, but also especially to those who have not been thinking in this direction merely because of the lack of models and/or encouragement."

Reverend Grant's work in the church began at an early age when, as one of nine children of the Reverend and Mrs. Joseph J. Grant, she was brought up in the church's youth activities and organizations in her native Georgetown, South Carolina. She graduated as salutatorian of her class at Howard High School (1966) and went on to obtain her Bachelor's degree in French and music from Bennett College, Greensboro, North Carolina. During her third year in college she decided that she would study for the ministry, as a culmination of all her church and community work and, as she said, the realization, "that the rest of my life was meant to be devoted to God's work through the church, not only as a natural function, but as a purposeful and structured one."

Therefore, she entered Turner Theological Seminary at the Interdenominational Theological Center in Atlanta, Georgia, where she completed requirements for and received the Master of Divinity degree, *cum laude*. Currently, Reverend Grant is working on her doctorate in systematic theology at Union Theological Seminary in New York City. She is also serving as an associate minister at Allen A.M.E. Church in Jamaica, New York.

Although she finds that being Black, a woman, young and educated in the institutional Church is threatening to many people, creating obstacles for her, she takes these obstacles as challenges, and therefore appeals to her inner strength, both intellectually and emotionally, to overcome them.

Profiles in Black

Employee Counselor
JOSEPH M. WARREN
New York, New York

In September 1972, Joseph M. Warren was one of three Blacks to be given a civil service award in New York City for his work as director of employee counseling with the Metropolitan Transit Authority. The citation read: "Through his efforts, the program has enlisted a wide variety of social services in the community. His expertise has led many public and private groups throughout the country to seek his help in setting up such programs."

The program cited was the counseling of employees who have alcoholic problems. Through his past personal experience with alcoholism, Joe Warren has brought the rehabilitation of problem employees to the Transit Authority and has set up programs to counter this type of industrial alcoholism. He says, "When a supervisor shields an unfit employee, or secretly sends him home, it may make the supervisor feel like a good guy but this approach will simply delay the arrival of the 'moment of truth' which only objective confrontation achieves for the problem drinkers."

Warren's coworkers at the MTA are grateful for and enthused about the success of his work, stating that they would want a chance to repay his "invaluable gift to us and others...the gift of LIFE. Mr. Warren has been a pioneer in the field of industrial alcoholism and (he also) untiringly gives of himself in his own Bedford Stuyvesant community and Black areas . . . without ever expecting anything in return. Thousands of lives have been positively affected through his efforts."

The TA's Employee Counseling service, begun in 1956, had Joe Warren as the director for the past ten years. His major challenge is the aforementioned well-meaning but misguided supervisors whose attitudes he and his staff work to change in order for them to facilitate referrals to the service. Determination of alcoholism in the client is carefully done through work performance (or lack of it) and blood test by the TA lab. A reading of a .5 will usually show alcohol in the bloodstream. His program "offers the alcoholic a chance to do something constructive about his problem." Since Joe Warren and his staff never moralize, the employee is never taken to task. Discouraging the use of hospitilization insurance at the TA, his department advances money instead for a five-day stay at Mt. Carmel Guild Hospital in Paterson, New Jersey, and the employee signs a simple IOU. Joe Warren and his staff also do a lot of work with the family of the alcoholic. In the post-hospital period, the employee is expected to attend Alcholics Anonymous meetings as well as receive support from his or her family. The case record of the service began at 119 in 1956 and rose to 264 in 1971 and of 220 on an annual program approximately 40 recovered alcoholics have received promotions in their jobs and an additional 120 have been successful. Repeaters, however, have been re-indoctrinated in the program or, as a last resort, asked to leave their jobs.

This dynamic, effectual service counselor continues to give orientation classes to supervisors as well as set up programs for other community organizations on combating alcoholism. He has set up a similar program for the New York City Fire Department. Among the numerous associations and groups that have tapped Mr. Warren's expertise are Mt. Carmel Freeport, Kings County, Bellevue and Doctors hospitals; Union-Pacific Railroad Company, Omaha, Nebraska; L & N Railroad, Louisville, Kentucky; Hughes Aircraft Company; Canadian Forces and the Department of National Revenue, Ontario; U.S. Army, Fort Meade, Maryland; Hewlitt-Packard, Palo Alto, California, etc.

This impressive list of groups that Mr. Warren has aided through his carefully thought-out program has undoubtedly salvaged many broken homes and broken employees. The existence of his service should be an inspiration and guide to a soluble problem.

Mr. Warren is married and he and his wife have two children.

Early Childhood Educator
MARGARET SINGLETON DARDEN
Miami, Florida

Although Margaret Singleton Darden had always been interested in early childhood education, her job career began as a secretary for Dade County's 4-H Clubs, an organization dealing with children 10 to 18 years old. In 1971, she was an administrative assistant for State Representative Gwendolyn Cherry. Two years later Ms. Darden became a television reporter and producer for WPBT in North Miami Beach, Florida.

Ms. Darden's career in early childhood education began in 1966 with the Child Opportunity Programs sponsored by the Economic Opportunity program. She was dissatisfied with the teaching techniques because they did not promote a positive self-concept in the child and the curriculum was not child-oriented. She says, "learning was fun when I was a child and for some strange reason the children in this program just weren't getting the joys of learning."

She took early childhood courses at Miami-Dade Community College, South Campus, and in 1968 she became the director of Brownsville Child Opportunity Center. There she "had the opportunity to supervise teachers and express her ideas on the kind of atmosphere and teaching techniques which would allow children to get a good feeling about themselves, to develop an eagerness for learning through exploration and discovery."

Currently, she is a program coordinator for Dade County's Division & Child Development Services. She monitors and evaluates 11 day-care centers, 42 family day-care homes (infant care) and 4 after-school care programs, all of them government subsidized. She helps to develop curriculum, provide in-service training for staff and generates parent involvement in these programs.

Margaret Darden is a member of the State Child Care Advisory Council, which recently completed setting minimum standards for all child care facilities in Florida. This state law is one she drafted while she was Representative Cherry's administrative aide. In addition to this, she serves as a consultant for the Social and Economic Services that involves setting up workshops on early childhood development throughout the state. She has conducted several workshops for SFACUS (South Florida's Association Children Under Six) and other community organizations requesting her services. She is also a member of the City of Miami's Child Care Task Force and other state and national organizations.

Because she thinks that unused minds are a waste, it is her intention to give directors, teachers and parents the necessary tools to help "our young children develop into creative, thinking productive citizens."

Ms. Darden was born in Alamo, Georgia, in 1942. Her early school years—kindergarten through third grade—were spent at Cory in Detroit,

Profiles in Black

Michigan. She received her Associate of Arts from Miami-Dade Community College, South Campus, and completed another year at the University of Miami in Coral Gables, Florida. Presently a senior, she intends to graduate at the end of 1976.

Employment Agent, Restaurateur
WILLIAM HICKS, JR.
Cleveland, Ohio

Making history in the employment world is William Hicks, Jr. vice president-treasurer of RAN Associates, a minority employment agency located in Cleveland, Ohio. William Hicks became interested in employment agencies after successfully gaining employment himself through an agency.

Bill, as he is often called, spent ten years working at the University Hospital in Cleveland. Starting out as a dishwasher, he was promoted to supervisor of porters a year later. Being a very ambitious man, he was soon promoted to production manager of the food service department. Later he became manager of the cafeteria. Soon outgrowing that position, Hicks went to an employment agency where he secured a position which required him to manage two cafeterias, a snack shop and all campus catering at Case Western Reserve University in Cleveland.

While he was working in food service, Bill Hicks employed almost 3,000 people that included a large number of overqualified minorities. For example, there were college graduates who were employed as porters. Hicks began to challenge the "system" and to help provide growth and promotion in industry for qualified people. He teamed up with Norman Thomas and Ernest Jones, Jr. After much hard work at planning and training, the three opened the doors of RAN.

RAN Associates endeavors to provide an outlet for the talent that exists in the community, to secure socio-economic growth while aiding industries with much needed clerical and middle-management assistance. Business and industry operating in today's environment cannot afford to overlook such a valuable resource. The Fortune 500 and other "Blue Chip" companies have sought assistance from RAN. RAN is an applicant-oriented service that does not charge the applicant any fee. Running the agency at first was not easy and mistakes were made. But RAN grew and William Hicks grew with it. He handles the accounting, recruiting and placement responsibilities, plus office supervision.

To provide the Black community with some type of social outlet, Mr. Hicks opened his own restaurant and night club in 1975 in downtown Cleveland, the Second Stage. It offers lunches daily, plus professional catering for private parties, small weddings, conferences, luncheons and buffets. The lounge provides opportunities for young unknown entertainers to display their talent and, hopefully, the exposure would help them to be discovered.

William Hicks feels that the combination of an employment agency for job and career growth and the restaurant-lounge that provides social entertainment are two ways he can help the Black community progress. Busy as he is, he still finds time to spend with disadvantaged children.

Profiles in Black

Radio Station General Manager
DOROTHY EDWARDS BRUNSON
New York, New York

Dorothy Brunson, communications pioneer, overcame tremendous odds against achieving position and influence within the closed ranks of the mass media business, not only because she is Black but a woman as well. Thus, it was a milestone when H. Carl McCall, of Inner City Broadcasting Corporation, announced the appointment of Ms. Brunson as the first female general manager in the country.

Profiles in Black

With the advent of the Sixties, Ms. Brunson became a prime mover in the field of communications, a time when there were few Blacks in advertising. Her career is distinguished by her successful efforts in developing Black ad agencies to the point where they were finally accepted as an integral part of the industry.

As part-owner and vice president of marketing and media of both Howard Sanders Advertising and Eden Advertising and Communications, Ms. Brunson played a major role in attracting prominent national accounts to Black agencies for the first time in Madison Avenue history. This recognition and utilization of Black agencies was partly the result of the formation of the Afro-American Association of Advertising Agencies, of which Ms. Brunson is a founder.

Ms. Brunson also served as assistant general manager of radio station WWRL, the New York based Sonderling station, for three years.

A frequent guest on television and radio shows dealing with the business world, Ms. Brunson has earned a place in the 1973 volume of *Who's Who in Advertising*. She has continued to develop in the three areas in which she has spent her career: business management, advertising and public relations and Black economic development.

She keeps perpetually busy conducting seminars and workshops, and making speeches at local colleges. She is a member of many professional organizations, including the board of directors of New York Market Radio Advertising Broadcasters, Inc. (NYMRAD), an organization of executives from within the radio industry—sales managers through presidents. Ms. Brunson is the only woman among 400 members.

In accounting for her success, Ms. Brunson comments, "Of vital importance in maintaining and meeting the day-to-day challenges is the continuance of my learning experiences," citing further that she is "preparing to take graduate courses at New York University."

As for the future, she believes "that broadcasting in Africa will offer new opportunities and challenges."

Architect
JAMES RICHARD DOMAN, JR.
New York, New York

James Richard Doman, Jr., is the founder of Doman & Associates, an architectural firm established in 1967 to provide services to public and private clients, constructing housing, commercial buildings, community, health-care and educational facilities within the New York metropolitan area. Mr. Doman and his staff of eight perform services such as: concept and development in construction technology; research and program development; feasibility studies; administration of construction; interior architecture including the research, selection, purchase and supervision of installation of the materials.

James Doman is a native New Yorker who obtained his undergraduate degree in architecture from Pratt Institute in 1965 and his Master's degree in architecture from Columbia University in 1971. He has a strong philosophy about Blacks in architecture: "Black people are considerably different in life-style, thinking and experiences from white people." However, he believes that a definition of Black architecture has not been arrived at because "there are few Blacks involved in architecture, and only a small percentage of these think about things Black architecturally.... We are attempting to identify and design this form."

Doman thinks that architects are artists who act as pointers toward a direction of hope. And through the practice of their profession architects become a very meaningful social force. He advises that anyone going into the profession of architecture must personally recognize the egotistical way in which human beings tend to behave. Honest understandings of that tendency in the architect can contribute immeasurably to success. Success, he feels, is a combination of honesty, arrogance, ego and desire. "It is the ability to dictate, corral and harness the activities of more than one individual."

This inspiring professional has taught at Columbia University, New York University, the Opportunities Industrialization Center and the Architects Renewal Committee in Harlem. James Doman is currently Professor of Architecture at the City College (City University of New York) School of Architecture and Environmental Studies. He is listed in *Who's Who in the East* and *Community Leaders of America.*

Profiles in Black

...I think all theories are suspect, that the finest principles may have to be modified, or may even be pulverized by the demands of life, and that one must find, therefore, one's own moral center and move through the world hoping that this center will guide one aright. I consider that I have many responsibilities, but none greater than this: to last, as Hemingway says, and get my work done. I want to be an honest man and a good writer.

—James Baldwin

Essayist, Novelist (Go Tell It on the Mountain, Notes of a Native Son, Giovanni's Room, others)

Community Leader
ROSETTA GASTON
Brooklyn, New York

The daughter of migrants from North Carolina, Rosetta Gaston was born in 1885 in a tenement in New York City. At that time, there were about 6,000 Blacks living in lower Manhattan, the "Stag District," and the wages for Blacks averaged five dollars per week.

Her father, a minister with the African Methodist Episcopal Church, died when she was nine. At fourteen, she had to leave school to help support the family by hanging coats and dusting pianos at John Wanamaker's for four years. For two years she worked at Gimbel Brothers at eight dollars per week, then for the next forty years at Bergdorf Goodman starting as an elevator operator at twelve dollars per week. Her career began as an organizer when she advocated better pay for four other Blacks working in the company some of whom are currently in important positions. She also engaged in community activities for the YWCA.

In 1939, she founded the Kipirsi Society for the Study of Black History. In the early Forties, she met a teacher in Harlem, the late Harcourt A. Tynes, who interested her in the New York branch for the study of Negro Life and History, and who was to have an immediate influence on her career. In 1943, she met Dr. Carter G. Woodson, who inspired her to work for the national organization. Two years later, with Dr. Woodson's permission, she formed the first Carter G. Woodson Club. She also organized the Brooklyn branch of the organization. With the help of Carrie L. Smith and Gertrude P. McBrown (see profile), an outstanding Negro history program was arranged at Siloam-Presbyterian Church with Dr. John Hope Franklin as guest speaker. The program was given to present contributions raised from her fellow workers at Bergdorf Goodman for the Association. She also received strong moral encouragement for her work from another famous national leader, Mrs. Mary McCloud Bethune.

At age 76, Rosetta Gaston organized the Brownsville branch in 1962. She remembers, "One of the highlights in my life was having the New York City Housing Authority name the Senior Citizens development complex The Carter G. Woodson Houses, a living symbol of his great work for his people." Later the Brownsville Community Council named the Senior Citizen Center after her.

She adds, "The Carter G. Woodson Houses and Community Center were dedicated in May 1971. In our present Brownsville branch, some of the original members of the Carter G. Woodson Club still carry on the work of the organization and strive in every way to help me realize my dream that someday the youths will have a building like the senior citizens." On her 91st birthday, at a tribute to this dedicated and energetic lady, pledges were made to make this last particular dream of Rosetta Gaston's materialize, adding to her credits of generating programs in her community for senior citizens as well as youth, and making these programs a reality.

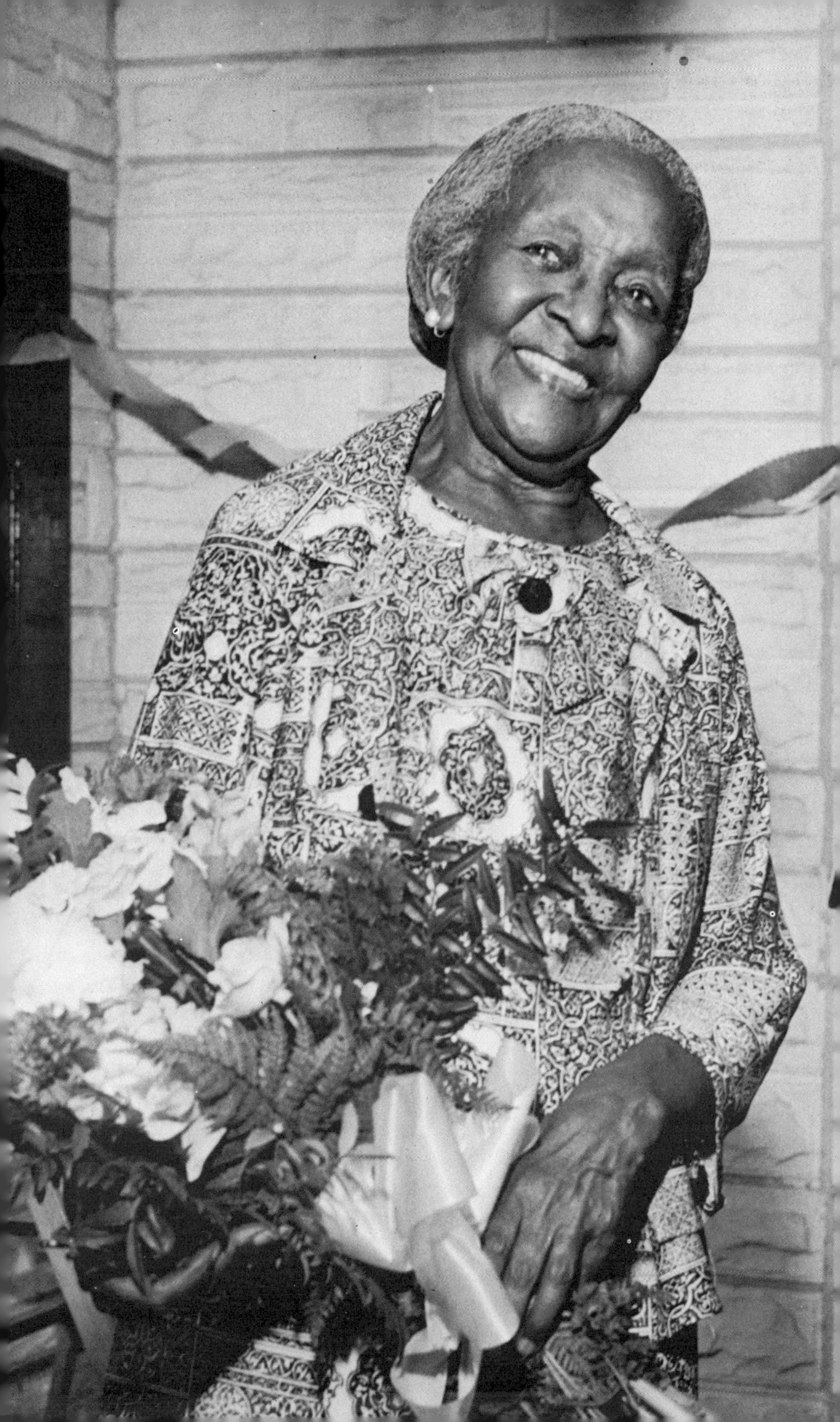

Obstetrician/Gynecologist
ERROLL BYER
Brooklyn, New York

In 1974, Erroll Byer began his career as a doctor after fifteen years of persistent preparation. His success story began in 1956 when he moved to New York from his birthplace, St. George Parish in Barbados.

After graduating from high school, Byer was employed as a cook in the kitchens of Kings County Hospital Center. While attending evening courses at the City College of New York in 1961, he applied for a volunteer job at Kings County Hospital Center's Blood Bank. The director of the blood bank took an instant interest in young Erroll, who he felt certain had the fortitude and determination to go much further than blood banking. The director's confidence was to be fulfilled.

In 1966, Byer changed his major from chemistry to medical technology and passed the civil service exam for a position as a laboratory aide. He also earned an Associate of Arts degree in applied sciences from New York City Community College. Two years later he passed the required exam to become a laboratory technician and later laboratory supervisor. The same director of Kings County Blood Bank was the one who encouraged him to take the latter exam.

In 1967, he was involved in the research and discovery of the Augustine Blood Group at Kings County Hospital Center. Only five people in the world had this particular blood type and like other rare blood types it was named after the mother and child in whom the type was first discovered.

Erroll Byer obtained his Bachelor of Science degree in 1969 from Richmond College, Staten Island. As a full-time student he worked evenings at Cumberland Hospital Blood Bank and on weekends at Kings County Blood Bank. Upon receiving his degree, he was promoted to junior bacteriologist at Kings County and worked there until June 1974.

In 1969, Byer was awarded the Jonas Salk Scholarship by the City University of New York for original research. He decided to apply to medical school. In September 1970, Erroll Byer was accepted at Downstate Medical College. While working his way through medical school he continued working weekends at Kings County.

Dr. Byer's advice to young poeple interested in the medical field is that "If something is dear to you, it matters little how much time it takes to achieve a particular goal. What is important is that you are willing to commit yourself to this achievement."

Profiles in Black

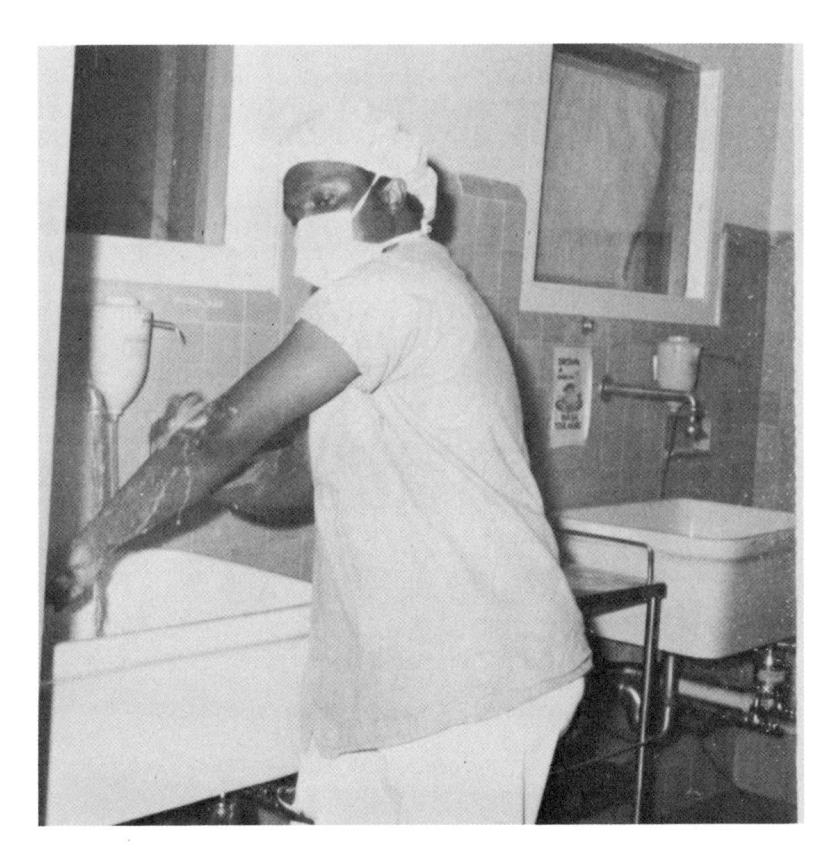

Founder of Black Awareness Schools
GERTRUDE WILKS
East Palo Alto, California

Gertrude Wilks, her husband Otis and their three children were among the earliest Black settlers in East Palo Alto, California. Mrs. Wilks was a dressmaker at that time and frequently discussed current issues with her clients as she fitted their dresses. She has always been committed to community struggles. As her children entered and passed through public schools, education became her main thrust "to end the destruction of Black youth and to build, from within, a proud Black community." And that was the *raison d'etre* for Mothers of Equal Education, a group that was the prototype to the Nairobi Schools that Mrs. Wilks founded.

Gertrude Wilks was born in Louisiana to a preacher/sharecropper, the Reverend Roosevelt Dyer, and to a wonderfully cheerful and competent mother, Eula Dyer. The Dyer household was always the hub of the plantation community, the predecessor of the Wilks residence that always seemed to be "smack in the middle of the Nairobi Schools."

Young Gertrude graduated from high school only because she successfully sneaked off to school every day without the "boss" finding out until she had established herself as a student. Her determination has persisted until today, centering around education for Black children and building up the Black community.

Mrs. Wilks personifies Nairobi—the school's strength and power, its faith and brilliance. She has served on innumerable boards of directors at Nairobi. She has worked for the Ravenswood City school district and the local high school PTA. She has been president of her church missionary society. She tried to "integrate" youngsters into several white school districts, an attempt that was mildly successful. She has been an educational consultant to Housing and Urban Development (HUD) Agency and to the Wright Institute as well as to various other high schools and colleges. She is currently the Director of the Nairobi Day School, Nairobi High School, the Annette Latorre Nursery School and the Saturday Day School, which is centrally located in the Black community of East Palo Alto. Instead of acting merely as a supplement to our homogeneous educational system where Black students are often badly counseled, the Nairobi Schools become an alternative, with a curriculum oriented toward Black self-awareness and respect.

Born out of courage and desperation, the Nairobi Schools have succeeded. They have brought beauty to the community that might never have been conceived without Gertrude Wilks.

Profiles in Black

Aeronautical Engineer
O.S. WILLIAMS
Jamaica, New York

O.S. Williams began a challenging and fulfilling career in aeronautics during World War II, when, armed with an aeronautical engineering degree from New York University, he boldly strode into the Republic Aviation plant that was heavily guarded and protected with barbed wire, and announced that he had an appointment with Dr. A. Alexander Kartveli, the famous aircraft designer. The guards quizzically escorted Williams past two checkpoints to Dr. Kartveli's office, where Williams's bluff was almost called. The renowned designer, recognizing that the young graduate student was taking a gambit in applying for a job, aided him in obtaining a position as a junior design engineer, the first Black to be hired to such a position. Within four years he became senior aerodynamicist, having earned a Master's in aeronautical engineering.

The second part of Williams's career started in 1956 when he was employed at Greer Hydraulics, manufacturers of aircraft accessories. After six years of working in the aeronautical field, he felt the urge to move into a more challenging area—like rocketry. With the support and help of Ed Greer, president of the company, O.S. Williams was placed with Reaction Motors Division of Thiokol Chemical Corporation, where he became a specialist in small rocket-engine design within six years. In that period he presented technical papers on spacecraft control rockets at the annual meetings of the American Rocket Society, now known as the American Institute of Aeronautics and Astronautics.

Williams joined Grumman Aerospace Corporation in 1961 as a rocket propulsion engineer, specializing in liquid fuels. Seven years later, he and two other Black engineers formed "Big Brother," the minority self-help organization whose aims were to force acknowledgment and upgrading of unused potential of minorities on the company payroll. "With the support of the Long Island chapter of CORE, we confronted company management repeatedly until a fair degree of minority upward mobility was accomplished." Grumman's Black employees wrote the affirmative action plan with the guidance of Mr. O.S. Williams, who had since become proficient as a task force leader in the Government/Industry Plan for Progress to motivate students in predominantly Black colleges to prepare themselves for business and technology.

In 1973, he broached the subject of company investment in West Africa to the president of Grumman, whose reaction was favorable. Mr. Williams was assigned market-survey missions to Nigeria, to visit 8 of their 12 states, and to establish Grumman's African headquarters there. As vice president of Grumman International, he states, "Being Black is probably an advantage to my new post—to Nigerians—but I am also an American businessman."

Profiles in Black

O. S. Williams, left, discusses aircraft-wiring design with Nigerian engineer L. Okunola, center, and Grumman foreman E. Jenkins, right.

He attributes his success to the philosophy that he promotes to young people: "(1) work hard to be prepared for the breaks when they come, (2) volunteer for the tough jobs with increasing responsibility and (3) never give up on yourself."

Writer, Magazine Editor
HOYT W. FULLER
Chicago, Illinois

Hoyt W. Fuller, born in Atlanta, Georgia, received his early education in Detroit, Michigan. He did his undergraduate work at Wayne State University, Detroit, and post-graduate work in English literature at the same school.

He worked as editor and reporter for many publications. He was with the *Detroit Tribune,* the *Michigan Chronicle, Ebony* magazine and the *Haagse Post,* Amsterdam, the Netherlands, as its West African correspondent. He was the executive editor of *Black World* (formerly *Negro Digest),* a periodical that he built into a prestigious, internationally circulated and widely read journal of ideas and Black culture.

Hoyt Fuller's sense of social awareness sharpened, he says, "at the beginning of the Sixties, when I came to understand that my life's work would have to revolve around increasing the consciousness and the sense of history of Black people." He was a founder of the Organization of Black American Culture (OBAC) in Chicago in 1967, an important cultural unit that produced the famous "Wall of Respect" and launched a mural movement in the U.S. He remains chairman of OBAC and advisor to the OBAC Writers Workshop which has contributed to the Black literary renaissance of the Sixties and Seventies. As editor *par excellence,* Hoyt Fuller has given much needed encouragement to young Black writers and has contributed immeasurably to the Black literary scene through his lectures, travels and writing.

His travels in Europe and especially North and West Africa and three months' residence in newly independent Guinea in 1959 led to the writing of a book, *Journey to Africa.* Hoyt Fuller also gained a John Hay Whitney Opportunity Fellowship in 1965 to travel and study in Africa.

From these travels and studies his philosophy evolved into the issues of educating Black people to "break out of the bind which Black Americans have been trapped in" by making themselves aware of the "nature of the society of which they are a part and . . . the ceaseless need to resist that society and, ultimately, to destroy it."

He continues, "It is my feeling that it is the duty of any Black individual who would represent Black people to struggle endlessly to inform Black people that they can never truly be "accepted" into racist America and it is clearly the duty of those Black individuals to lead their people to continually encourage Black people to reject the American system and to organize their lives and emotions around values of humanity and community. I consider it my responsibility to inform Black people of routes to fulfillment which do not coincide with the American ethic."

Profiles in Black

Space Program Administrator
RUTH BATES HARRIS
Washington, D.C.

Ruth Bates Harris began her career with membership on a panel that directed the affairs of Alcorn College in Mississippi, during the absence of the president. Later she became the first Black secretary with the Philip Morris Company in New York. In Washington, D.C., from 1960-69, she served with the Human Relations Commission as assistant director, deputy director and executive director in which capacity she was the first Black and first woman director.

Mrs. Harris has advised and assisted the former Board of Commissioners—presidential appointees who manage the affairs of the nation's capital—and later the mayor of Washington, as a member of his cabinet. She ordered the first public hearing into equal employment opportunity discrimination in the government of the District of Columbia. Her efforts brought both jobs and promotions to hundreds of Blacks and other minorities as well as women. Her Human Relations and Police Community Relations training and other programs have been widely hailed throughout the U. S.

Ruth Bates Harris was born in Washington, D.C., although she grew up in New York City. She received her Bachelor of Science degree from Florida A & M University and her Master's in Business Administration from New York University. She majored in personel administration and industrial relations at the latter.

She is the author of three publications: *Handbook for Careerists,* a guide for youths preparing for and seeking jobs, later reprinted by the Washington Metropolitan Board of Trade; *Employer's Handbook on Merit Employment,* reprinted by the U.S. Employment Service; and *Trigger Words,* a compendium of words to avoid when addressing others. The latter volume has been used by federal and local government people and various police jurisdictions.

She was the first director of human relations for the Montgomery County Public Schools from 1969-71, in which capacity she developed a policy statement and program for action for 126,000 students and 6,000 teachers. In October 1971, she became the first director of the Equal Employment Opportunity in the National Aeronautics and Space Administration. On April 1973, she was named Deputy Assistant Administrator, the first woman in NASA to hold that position.

In October 1973, she was dismissed from NASA after she co-authored a private report to NASA's administrator, criticizing the agency's equal opportunity effort. Hundreds of protestors sent letters and telegrams which resulted in three congressional hearings. With the aid of her attorneys and the NAACP Legal Defense Fund, an amicable agreement was made and she was reinstated to a new position of Deputy Assistant Administrator for Community and Human Relations in August 1974.

She has received many awards and citations for her efforts on behalf of the community. She is listed among prominent Black Americans in publications of the Association for the Study of Afro-American Life and History.

Ruth Bates Harris is married to an electrical engineering consultant and they have four children.

Historian
CHANCELLOR WILLIAMS
Washington, D.C.

Chancellor Williams was born in Bennetsville, South Carolina, where his elementary education was completed at the Marlboro Academy before his family moved to Washington, D.C. He attended Dunbar High School and Armstrong High School, graduating from the latter and obtained a B.A. in education from Howard University and a M.A. in history in 1935. He also did post-graduate, nonresident studies at the University of Chicago and the University of Iowa and earned his Ph.D from The American University in 1949.

From 1953-54, Dr. Williams was Visiting Research Scholar at Oxford University, England, and the University of London where formal research in African history began at Rhodes House, the British Museum and later at museums in Paris and Italy where one can see the vast scale on which Africa has been raped of so much of her early culture.

In 1956, he began direct field studies in African history, based at University College which later became the University of Ghana. The main objective of the field research was to determine precisely the independent achievements of the African race and the nature of Black civilization before either Asian or European influence penetrated the continent. This required a continent-wide survey centering on traditional Africa. The first phase was completed in 1957. The final field studies covering 26 countries and 105 language groups were completed in 1964.

The career of Chancellor Williams has been wide and varied. He has been a businessman (president of Log Cabin Wholesale Baking Co.), an editor *(The New Challenge),* a cooperative organizer (vice president and general manager of Cooperative Industries, Inc.), a U.S. government economist, a teacher of the D.C. high schools; a school principal in Maryland; a historical novelist *(The Raven, Have You Been to the River?,* etc.), and author-historian *(The Rebirth of African Civilization, The Destruction of Black Civilization,* etc.), and a university professor. The *Destruction of Black Civilization* has been given the 1971 Book Award by the Black Academy of Arts and Letters. He has two works in progress: *Black Odyssey,* about the destruction of African civilization in Egypt and the Sudan and *The Second Agreement With Hell,* that covers the last years of slavery in the U.S. to Blacks' first entry in politics.

In 1971, Dr. Williams was honored when the Howard University History Club renamed the history department The Chancellor Williams Historical Society. He received a special presentation from The Sons and Daughters of Africa in 1974.

Profiles in Black

Physical Therapist
BRENDA WALKER
New York, New York

Third in line of six girls and one boy in a Brownsville, Brooklyn family, Brenda Walker had always been a different child who made high academic achievements and participated in diverse extracurricular activities such as dancing, artwork and the glee club. She was, in her words, "bookish and withdrawn" as an adolescent. Because of the family religion, they were known as the "Black Jews of Brownsville." When she was about 11, her parents separated and her mother had to rely on public assistance to support the family.

Brenda Walker proved to be equally successful in her high school career as she recalls, "My greatest achievement in high school was when I received the Lincoln Center Student Award for academic excellence and appreciation of the arts." The prize was a year's worth of tickets to the performing arts, from operas to plays. In her senior year she moved to her grandmother's where the atmosphere was more conducive to study. After graduation she got a civilian personnel job on Governor's Island and work in the Manpower Program won her a commendation from former President Lyndon B. Johnson.

She was accepted to New York University as a physical-therapy major, and, although she knew that her family could hardly afford the tuition, her mother signed the installment plan papers. They received no aid from public assistance after she started college, so that in a nervous, depressed and tearful state, she went to see the student finance officer. Shortly after, based on her excellent scholarship record, she became a recipient of grants, loans and scholarship incentive awards from the University, and was able to live in a dormitory.

A year later she joined the staff of The Rusk Institute, part of NYU Medical Center.

She worked next at Beekman Downtown Hospital in a small rehabilitation department, then at the New York chapter of United Cerebral Palsy as part of a team housed in the Willowbrook State School, Staten Island. Her team was the first professional staff the school encountered. The lack of staff and knowledge at Willowbrook was pointed out in newscaster Geraldo Rivera's expose. There she had the chance to take a special course in neurodevelopmental technique, on how to deal with brain-injured children. She later obtained a Master's in special education from NYU. Currently, she is on New York City's Board of Education's Pre-placement Center for the multiple-handicapped child. As the sole physical therapist, she works with two teachers and paraprofessionals in the training and teaching of these special children and in working with the children's families. Brenda Walker also gives professional help to the Industrial Home for the Blind.

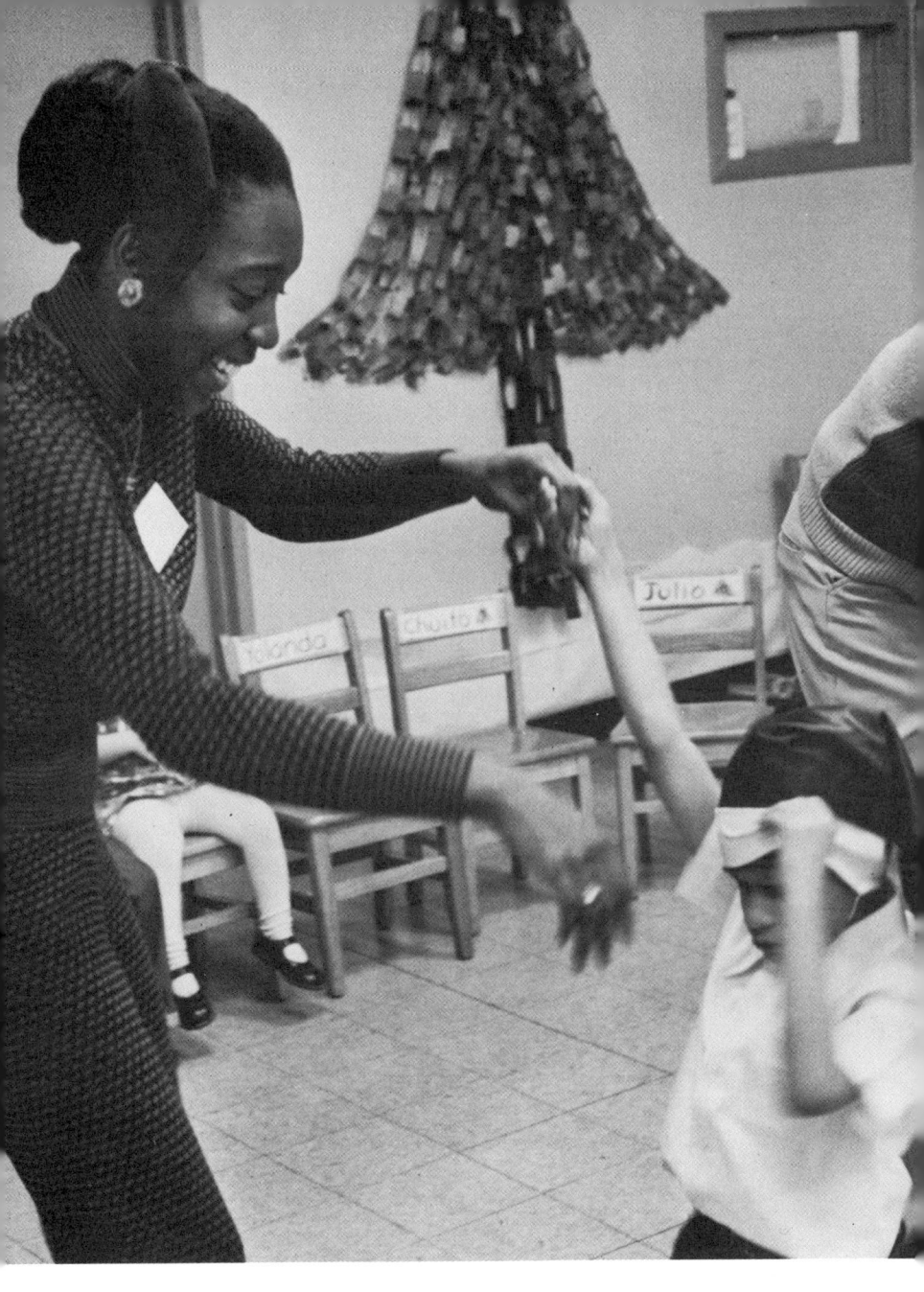

She hopes to become a child specialist, continuing to work with the brain-damaged child as a pediatric physical therapist or consultant. Her philosophy is: "Any road is hard to travel, no matter who or what you are. If you believe in something higher than yourself and try to keep your mind and body in harmony, you'll make it to some point on this road, even if it is just to know and accept yourself."

Business Executive/Community Activist
LAWRENCE W. CARROLL
Chicago, Illinois

Lawrence W. Carroll was born on the South Side of Chicago, Illinois. When he was three his father died, leaving his mother, Lucille, and a brother to carry on the operation of a printing shop which his father had started. From the age of 9 to 20, Lawrence spent the bulk of his time in the printing business and ultimately managed it. It was a small operation grossing an average of ten thousand dollars a year in the early Forties and Fifties.

Carroll attended Herzl Junior College and received his Associate of Arts degree in 1942. He then attended the University of Illinois from 1942-44 at Champaign-Urbana, leaving four months before graduation to enter the Air Force where he became a pilot of multi-engine aircraft. After the war he returned to Chicago to attend Loyola University where he received his law degree in 1950.

Lawrence W. Carroll is one of the charter members of The Woodlawn Organization (often referred to as T.W.O.) of the early Sixties, which is one of the most renowned and sustaining community organizations in this country, geared to protecting residents of the Woodlawn area of Chicago. The Woodlawn population at that time was over 85,000. It was founded by the Woodlawn Pastor's Alliance with the help of the master organizer, the late Saul Allinski, of the Industrial Areas Foundation.

Today The Woodlawn Organization, over 15 years old, is the umbrella organization for over 115 community groups, businessmen's organizations, churches and block clubs. The early days of The Woodlawn Organization were filled with protests, picketing and battles with the power structure that included the initiation of the successful movement to "dump Ben Willis," the racially biased superintendent of Chicago schools, and the conciliation between the community and the University of Chicago, which halted the unwanted advance of the university into the Woodlawn community.

This organization—T.W.O.—combined with Hillman's Corporation, a food chain in the Midwest, to form a third corporation known as T.W.O./Hillman's Inc. T.W.O. is the proprietor of over 44 million dollars' worth of assets in its own community. Its motto is "Self Determination." The company's assets include 504 units of housing built in 1966, two thirds ownership of stock in T.W.O./Hillman's Corporation, a supermarket enterprise, a movie theatre, 322 units of housing and over 150 units of rehabilitation housing currently being completed. Lawrence Carroll now serves Chicago Title Insurance Company as office counsel. He was nominated president and chief executive officer of T.W.O./Hillman's Inc., in November 1970 and has served as its only chief executive. T.W.O./Hillman's grossed 4.2 million dollars in its fourth year of operation.

Lawrence Carroll is married and he and his wife have one son, **Lawrence Carroll III**.

Profiles in Black

Businesswoman
CHARLENE B. OWENS
Hattiesburg, Mississippi

Venturing into business was very rare for Blacks growing up in the South some 30 or 40 years ago. However, Mrs. Charlene B. Owens considers herself very fortunate because her father, now deceased, and her uncles had successfully entered various businesses and paved the way somewhat for her. Mrs. Owens's mother, now Mrs. Josephine Washington, taught at Mississippi's famed Piney Woods Institution.

Profiles in Black

Mrs. Owens attended Alcorn A & M University and a local business school which inspired her to urbanize Black facilities in her area. In 1957, she started a women's fashion salon, called the Style Shop, that carried the latest fashions. During that time the potential for success of a Black business was thought to be limited because of the economic status of Black people. Although she encountered many problems with the local chamber of commerce, she was ultimately very successful and the success of that business led her to venture into others: Shopper's World, Charlene's Realty, Golden Gate Funeral Home, Jerry's Modern Day Apartments and Jerry B. Owens Business & Professional Plaza—all of which she takes great pride in.

Mrs. Owens has three children, young adults following in her successful footsteps. Her son, Jerry, owns and operates a store for men located in Shopper's World. He is a graduate of Tennessee State University, Nashville. Her daughter, Johnnie Ruth, is a graduate of Southern University, Baton Rouge, Louisiana. She owns and operates a clothing store for women, also located in Shopper's World. The younger daughter, Judy, graduated from William Carey College, Hattiesburg, Mississippi, with a major in speech. She decided on a career in television and is currently a news reporter for WLBT, Mississippi's largest TV station.

Mrs. Owens hopes that her work and family dedication will inspire Blacks nationwide to seek business careers in order to upgrade the economic status of all of America's Black communities.

Fire Chief
JAMES H. SHERN
Pasadena, California

James Shern was born fifty years ago in Kansas City, Kansas, the middle son of three boys. His father was employed with the Santa Fe Railroad. After achieving an excellent record in high school, he entered the U.S. Army Signal Corps and later attended Kansas City Junior College. After a brief period of travel, fulfilling his wanderlust, he settled down to work and found his first job at a shipyard in Los Angeles and later a job as a sheet metal worker. Although in 1948 jobs were plentiful, raises in salary were not frequent. He saw an ad in the paper for a fireman's job in Los Angeles, took the exam and became one of the few Blacks in the fire department. He muses, "Without that combination of concern over low wages and just happening across the ad, there's no telling where I would have been today."

He returned to school in 1956 and obtained his Associate of Arts degree in chemistry from Los Angeles City College, while working as a senior inspector of fire prevention. In 1964, he received a Bachelor of Science degree from California State University at Los Angeles.

During his first six years of fire service, he worked with the dangerous chemical and industrial units, involving complex research and fire prevention. In 1961, Chief Shern aided in putting out the two-day Bel Air fire that did millions of dollars of damage to over 400 homes. From 1961-65, he instructed fire prevention at East Los Angeles College and at California State University at Long Beach. During this period he also did extensive research in studying the causes of fire and the design and structure of fire-proofing buildings. His findings are now part of the fire code published in 1965 by the National Fire Prevention Association, and a work published in 1966 for the American Society for Testing Materials.

Another fire crisis that Chief Shern encountered was on Friday the Thirteenth, August 1965, when on a smoggy morning he reported for duty at Fire Station 18, and for 36 hours was involved with helping to quell the Watts riot fires.

In February 1968, he was the first Black to be appointed battalion chief of the Los Angeles Fire Department. He served as chief for over a year, doing administration work in fire prevention and suppression areas. He went to Pasadena in 1972 to take a tune-up exam for an assistant chief's job in L.A. The tune-up route brought him to Pasadena where he took the fire chief's job. He recalls the outcome of the test, "When former Pasadena City Manager John Phillips called me the day after the exam to offer me the job, my first inclination was that the caller was one of my L.A. fire department friends playing a joke, until I met up with Phillips—and made the decision to accept the Pasadena post." Chief Shern became the first Black fire chief in a city of more than 100,00 population.

Profiles in Black

In performing his regular firefighting duties, he felt the need for an affirmative action program. "Pasadena was lagging behind in the hiring of minorities," he points out. "In an effort to correct this situation and to bring Pasadena in compliance with the Fair Employment Practices Act, we initiated a fire technician program." Because of the program, there was an increase in the hiring of minorities.

Chief Shern belongs to numerous civic organizations, and holds a position on the board of directors of the California Fire Chiefs Association. Governor Ronald Reagan appointed Shern to the State Board of Fire Service, which was established to standardize firefighting equipment and training.

Chief Shern is married and he and his wife, Mercedes, have one child.

History is the landmark by which we are directed into the true course of life. The history of a movement, the history of a nation, the history of a race is the guide-post of that movement's destiny, that nation's destiny, that race's destiny. What you do today that is worthwhile inspires others to act at some future time. (1923)

—Marcus Garvey

Black Nationalist Leader, the most successful organizer of Black people in the Western hemisphere

Communications Educator
DELORIS COSTELLO
New York, New York

As far back as the early Sixties, Deloris Costello communicated her concern over the progress—or lack of progress—of Blacks in the media. While doing research for an article for *TV Guide,* she felt certain that television and radio "were going to open to Black people who wanted to make a meaningful and intelligent contribution."

The decrease in the number of Black reporters working for the major networks—from a high of 200 in 1964 to approximately 6 that are currently members of the Association of Radio and Television News Analysis Union—changed Ms. Costello's earlier optimism. She was convinced that the objective of the establishment media was to pacify and entertain. The cancellation of TV and radio programs she considered relevant to Black communities added further weight to her charges.

Ms. Costello was employed at New York's WBAI, a listener-supported, noncommercial radio station, when she founded Third World Communications Vanguard. She brought Black and Puerto Rican youths to the station to teach them to report, announce and produce radio programs. A workshop was set up to teach them to operate, control and manage the communications equipment that "would ultimately control their lives."

The aim of the volunteer-staffed TWCV is to focus programs on Third World communities in an effort to project news on the social, political and economic struggles of Third World people. Most programs are bilingual, primarily English and Spanish. While musical programs are included in TWCV's formula, Ms. Costello faults other so-called soul stations who she says have only two aims "to lull Black people to sleep with music, and more music and to sell the white man's products."

Ms. Costello was appalled that in New York City not one station that supposedly serves the Black community aired such major events as the Nixon impeachment hearings, the Senate Watergate investigations, President Ford's press conferences or other events that affect Black people.

The Third World Communications Vanguard is now in its third year of operation. Under Deloris Costello's direction TWCV has ten programs to its credit and is setting an example for other media-oriented people who understand the importance of communications to the survival of Black people.

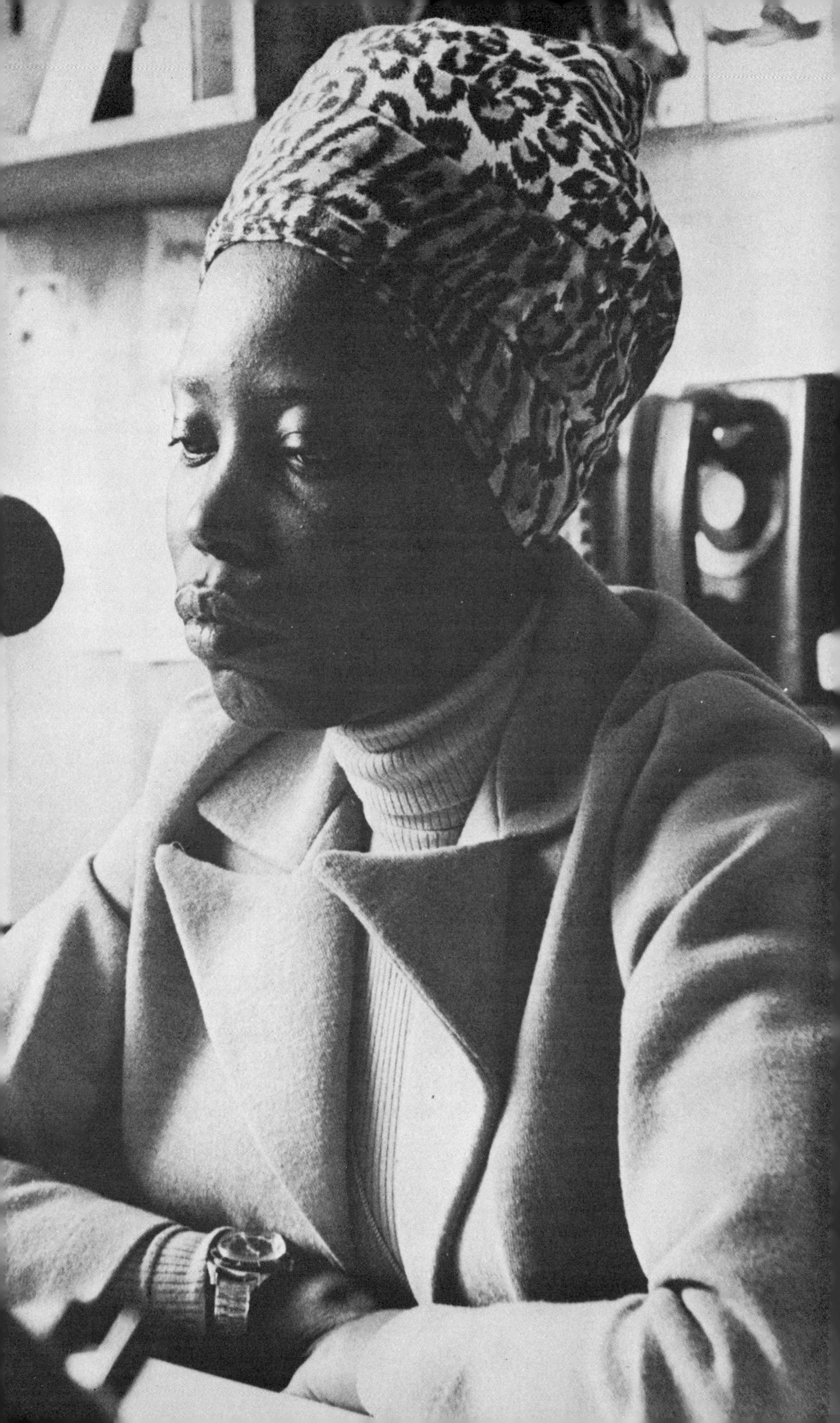

Sickle Cell Researcher
CHARLES F. WHITTEN
Detroit, Michigan

Charles F. Whitten's story does not focus on your usual "rags to riches" or "up the ladder" success story, but rather on a traditional family function by "bettering yourself through education."

Charles Whitten lost his father when he was ten years old. His mother, Emma C. Whitten, being the dynamic person that she was, served as a perfect example of endurance and determination to hurdle her plight in raising four children (the youngest was 22 months) toward a healthy and rewarding life. Mrs. Whitten taught school, took in sewing and dressed hair, managing successfully to keep her family together.

Charles Whitten had the desire to be a doctor from the age of six. And his education was geared in that direction when he received his Bachelor of Arts degree in 1942 from the University of Pennsylvania. He worked at home evenings to earn his spending money. He went on to attend Meharry Medical College and received his medical degree in 1945.

Dr. Whitten served his internship in Lackawanna Hospital, Lackawanna, New York, and Harlem Hospital in 1946. From 1953-54, Dr. Whitten attended the University of Pennsylvania Graduate School of Medicine, specializing in pediatrics and completing his residency at Children's Hospital in Buffalo, New York.

Seeking other intellectual areas in the medical field, he began to study various blood diseases. This research led him to conduct interviews on sickle cell disease, resulting in the formation of the National Association for Sickle Cell Disease (NASCD) which was organized in Racine, Wisconsin, on December 11, 1971, with the support of the Johnson Foundation. He is currently president of the association.

Along with his NASCD duties, he is Professor of Pediatrics at Wayne State University School of Medicine and is the program director of the University's Comprehensive Sickle Cell Center. He also is a member of many community associations as well as contributor to numerous publications.

Behind this inestimable man is his wife Eloise, a "professional volunteer," who devotes many hours to community organizations as policymaker. Despite their busy schedule, the Whittens have raised two daughters, Lisa, 18, and Wanda, 16.

Profiles in Black

Community Leader
MARY BOWERS
Florence, South Carolina

Mrs. Mary Bowers of Florence, South Carolina, in performing her role as mother to a young son growing up in the Black community, noticed how bored her son was becoming due to the lack of recreational facilities and activities in their community. To alleviate her son's boredom, she began to send him to other communities to take part in their activities. However, she was still concerned over the plight of other children around her who had nothing else to do but roam the streets. She confronted the other adults in the neighborhood with the problem. Some were interested but they were either too busy working or had no children of their own. Others did not seem to care.

Then the idea came to her to become a den mother. In this way she could help to occupy the boys and girls in her community when their school day had ended. She posed her idea to the other parents and the result was quite favorable.

Mrs. Bowers enrolled in a training course for Boy Scout activities to prepare for the responsibilities of offering constructive programs to children during their leisure hours. When she initiated the new programs she found that she was enjoying them as much as the kids were. She recalls, "Boys from other troops wanted to join mine, and when they reached the age to become a Scout, they did not want to leave my cub scout troop."

She was a den mother for two years, and was awarded the Silver Fawn citation for her inspiring work.

Mrs. Bowers did not stop with these projects. She felt assured that through her experiences she could help others in the community relate better to their children's needs. When women were granted the opportunity to be selected as Commissioners of the Boy Scouts, she applied and was accepted. Mrs. Bowers became the first female Commissioner of the Boy Scouts in the Pee Dee (Piedmont) area. She is a member of the Florence County Headstart Policy Council.

Profiles in Black

Youth Program Director
BOB D. DUREN
Long Beach, California

A drop-out, a juvenile delinquent and a former inmate in a California prison, Bob D. Duren, 31, has lived in Long Beach, California, since 1960 when his parents moved from Cleveland, Ohio.

Bob attended Long Beach Polytechnic High School, but his inquiring analytical mind became stifled by an education that could neither relate to his immediate environment nor stimulate his personal interest. Like so many other young people today, at 17 he dropped out—or was pushed out of school—and took to the streets. He earned a sentence of five years to life for armed robbery. Instead of allowing himself to be programmed for a future life of crime, Bob utilized his time of confinement to develop a profound awareness of himself and the cause of his imprisonment. "These changes in my perspective on life," he says, "took place not because of the prison system but in spite of it." While in prison he completed not only his high school education but also several courses from the University of San Francisco.

When he returned to Long Beach in 1970, Bob was determined to change the adverse conditions that alienate and destroy the minds and spirits of many young people. Since 1971, he has been involved with many organizations that are concerned with the welfare and education of the people, such as the National Poor People's Congress, the Long Beach NAACP, the Central Area Neighborhood Council, the Experimental Educational Institute, Inc., the California Welfare Rights, among others.

Presently Bob is the director and teacher at the Intercommunal Youth Institute—a parent and community-controlled alternative school. Some of the subjects taught are World Awareness, emphasizing problems existing in our country that are connected worldwide; People's Health; Plant Care; People's History; Art and Music, teaching students to read music and to play instruments; Creative Writing; Vocabulary Development; Science; Math; Economics in Practical Usage; Community Awareness; Current Events; Spanish; and Crafts.

In 1973, with a small group of parents, he founded the Youth Institute, a unique community-controlled school that was recently included in the State Board of Education's 74-75 ESEA Title 1 Program. This program supplies federal monies to school districts for compensatory education for disadvantaged students. The Youth Institute serves parents and students who find public schools inadequate to their needs. Some students who have been "pushed out" of public schools are enrolled at the Youth Institute and have functioned well under a better environment.

This dynamic young man who started down a different avenue of life is actively working toward changing community values and exposing some of the myths which have perpetuated educational inequality.

Profiles in Black

Writer, Artist
MARGARET BURROUGHS
Chicago, Illinois

Margaret Burroughs, artist, author, curator and lecturer, was born in St. Rose, Louisiana, but moved to Chicago, Illinois, when she was four years of age. Mrs. Burroughs was educated in the public schools of Chicago and received her teacher's certificate from Chicago Normal College, her Bachelor's and Master's degrees in education from the Art Institute of Chicago and did her graduate work at Teacher's College at Columbia University, New York City.

Her diversified interest and restless spirit have found expression in a wide-ranging field of endeavors, from writing and illustrating children's literature to organizing art centers and helping to found, in 1959, the National Conference of Artists, an organization devoted to the growth and stimulation of art among Black people.

Her writing career has been distinguished by such works as *Jasper, the Drummer Boy; What Shall I Tell My Children?* and *Africa, My Africa,* a book of poetry, as well as two anthologies, *Did You Feed My Cow?* and *Whip Me Whop Me Pudding.*

Realizing the importance of community leadership and organization, Mrs. Burroughs, in 1939, was one of the founders of the Chicago South Side Community Art Center. Not content with the many projects for which she has been responsible, she and her husband, Charles, and others established in 1961 the DuSable Museum of African American History, one of the few museums of its kind in the country today.

In 1966, as an advisor of the National Conference of Artists, Dr. Burroughs was invited with a delegation of Black artists and writers to visit the Soviet Union. She has also traveled widely throughout Europe and Africa, sometimes exhibiting and lecturing during her travels.

While Dr. Burroughs has been the recipient of numerous rewards, including a doctorate of Humane Letters from Lewis University, Lockport, Illinois (1972) and the YMCA Leadership Award for Excellence in Art (1974), she has found unending rewards and pleasure through her continuing effort to deepen the artistic appreciation of persons, not only in Chicago, but wherever she can find an audience. It is her belief that "art breaks down barriers, racial and social," toward realizing total liberation.

Profiles in Black

Marine Operations Servicer
H. JUDE ALSANDOR
Lafayette, Louisiana

H. Jude Alsandor, a long-time resident of Acadiana, in the heart of Louisiana's French or "Cajun" country, began his career as a home builder and realtor after briefly attending the University of Southwestern Louisiana.

Mr. Alsandor has earned the respect of local folks as well as that of business throughout the coastal region because of his professional and civic performance. He can claim the distinction of having created the first minority-owned, offshore-oil servicing company of its type. In 1973, beginning with only four cooks and four utility men, Mr. Alsandor initiated what has grown into a million-dollar business, preparing and serving meals to workers on offshore oil rigs, providing general housekeeping services, and supplying rigs with personnel, foodstuffs, linens, cleaning and cooking supplies and equipment.

In 1975, Continental Catering saw the addition of two crew-cargo ships to their operation. The ships were financed by the Liberty Bank and Trust Company, a minority bank in New Orleans. The Interracial Council for Business Opportunity and the Acadiana Business and Economic Development Corporation were instrumental in packaging the loan.

Projections for this year place their gross sales around two million dollars, utilizing a staff of 96 employees. In addition to servicing seven offshore operations for AMOCO, Continental has secured contracts with Shell, Exxon, Chevron and Union Oil as well.

As one of Lafayette's leading businessmen and a well-known figure throughout the state of Louisiana, Alsandor sits on committees for the governor and a number of advisory boards in Lafayette.

Alsandor attributes his success to hard work. "Four or five hours of sleep is enough for me," said Alsandor. "I'm anxious for the next day to begin and excited about what challenges it will bring."

Profiles in Black

Cable TV Administrator
J. CLAY SMITH, JR.
Washington, D.C.

J. Clay Smith, Jr., is deputy chief of the Cable Television Bureau at the Federal Communications Commission, Washington, D.C. He is the first Black in the 40-year history of the Commission to be appointed to a policy staff position. He was formerly associated with the Washington, D.C., law firm of Arent, Fox, Kintner, Plotkin & Kahn, where he was engaged in antitrust and trade regulation matters. Mr. Smith is a native of Omaha, Nebraska. He received his B.A. degree from Creighton University, Omaha, in 1954, his J.D. degree from Howard University School of Law in 1967, his Master of Law degree from George Washington University

Profiles in Black

Law School in 1970 and has completed all course requirements on his doctorate of law (S.J.D.). His doctorate area of concentration is on Federal procedure.

Mr. Smith is a member of the District of Columbia, Nebraska, the National, the American and the Federal Bar Associations (F.B.A.). He is currently Council and Committee Coordinator of the F.B.A. and second vice president of the Washington Bar Association. He is a member of the National Conference of Black Lawyers, and active in The World Peace Through Law Center. He is a member of the Board of the Neighborhood Legal Service Program in Washington, D.C.

In 1974, he was chairman of the F.B.A.'s General Convention which was held in Washington, D.C. He has served as chairman of the F.B.A.'s tort law committee for two years, receiving an Outstanding Chairman Award for his service to the Association for both years. In September 1975, he was elected to the Executive Committee of the Federal Bar Association, becoming the first Black in the Association's history to be so honored. He serves as the Association's alternate to the House of Delegates of the American Bar Association. He served as managing editor of two issues of the Federal Bar Journal and has published more than 20 legal articles in leading national law journals and other publications. He is coauthor of a book on criminal law, *Criminal Defense Techniques.* recently Mr. Smith gave a speech that is reproduced in the Congressional Record entitled, "For A Strong Howard University Press." Other speeches by Mr. Smith have also been introduced for publication in the Record such as "Black Lawyers in the United States (1840-1900)."

During Mr. Smith's military service from 1967-71, he was a captain in the U.S. Army's Judge Advocate General's Corps, serving as a military judge from 1970-71. He received the Distinguished Service Award upon completion of his military service. He was an adjunct professor of law at Howard Law School for three years, and received, by vote of the law school student body, the Paul L. Diggs' Outstanding Law Professor Award in 1973. Mr. Smith has received several awards for his service in bar association activities.

He and his wife Olivia and their three children, Stager, 11, and nine-year-old twins Michael and Michelle, reside in Washington, D.C.

Television Advertising Producer
MARY RICHARDSON BROWN
Armonk, New York

Mary Richardson Brown, an identical twin, was born in Washington, D.C. She moved with her family to St. Louis, Missouri, her parent's native home, where Mary's father was dean of the Lincoln University School of Law. Nine years later the family moved to Washington, D.C., where at age 10 Mary edited a neighborhood newspaper. When her father was appointed to the federal bench in New York in 1957, the family moved to New Rochelle.

Ms. Brown produces corporate television commercials for IBM, from the world headquarters in Armonk, New York. Her first IBM commercial, "Navajo," won first prize in the "Image Building" category at the 1975 U.S. Television Commercials Festival. Before joining IBM, Mary was the foreign-syndication editor for network television for the American Broadcasting Company from 1972-74. In early 1972, she was a television newswriter with WNBC-TV and freelanced briefly for WPIX-TV. From 1970-71, she was a broadcaster and assistant promotion manager for KETV in Omaha, Nebraska, where she was host for a local talk show, "Rap About It." She has also been a reporter for the Baltimore Afro-American Newspaper, a guest editor of the Peace Corps News, and editor-in-chief of campus newspaper at Adelphi and Morgan State universities.

In the summer of 1974, she organized and taught a ten-week course in broadcast journalism at the Huguenot YMCA in New Rochelle. She researched and wrote the script for a documentary entitled, "Rape, Says Who?"—designed to inform women on how to report a rape attack—aired in 1975 on WOR-TV's "Straight Talk" program.

Mary Brown produced the First Annual New York Black Film Festival in New York City for the National Association of Media Women in June 1975, featuring the film and tape work of over 30 minority men and women, and will repeat her duties at an expanded Festival in May 1976. She has written plays for children and several feature film scripts which she hopes to compile into a book.

She holds a B.A. in political science from Morgan State University (1967) and a M.S. in broadcasting from the Columbia University Graduate School of Journalism (1972). For her project at Columbia, Ms. Brown wrote and produced a documentary on the New York City houses of detention and wrote a report on interviews with national Black leaders. Among her subjects were Congresswoman Shirley Chisholm, Vernon Jordan, Rev. Jesse Jackson, Roy Innis, the late Dr. George Wiley, Imamu Amiri Baraka and Mayor Kenneth Gibson.

Ms. Brown serves as financial secretary of the Metropolitan New York Chapter of the National Association of Media Women (NAMW) and is also a member of its National Board of Directors. She was cited by the

Profiles in Black

Metropolitan Chapter of the NAMW as 1976 Media Woman of the Year. She is a member of American Women in Radio and Television; the Society of Professional Journalists, Sigma Delta Chi; the Deadline Club; Writers Guild of America, East; the National Council on Crime and Delinquency; and the National Council of Negro Women.

Ms. Brown resides in New Rochelle with her parents, Judge Scovel Richardson of the U.S. Customs Court and Mrs. Richardson.

I was born June 25, 1850. This they called at that time "Corn plowing time." So when they designated my age, they would say: "He was born in corn plowing time, in, or about the year when the stars fell," or some incident of note.... A woman who had children regularly was called a "breeder" in those days.... My mother was a farm hand, and was considered a "breeder," so that in plowing time she worked right around her house, and plowed with an old horse by the name of "Selim."... My father lived three miles away. He would come in on Wednesday nights after things had closed up at his home, and be back at his home by daylight Thursday mornings; come again Saturday night, and return by daylight Monday morning. He had a pass weekly from his master that gave him this permission.... The night my mother died, I lay on a pallet next to a cradle and rocked my infant brother who was just five weeks old, and gave him the bottle all night. I did this when only nine years of age myself. (1924)

—William H. Heard

Teacher, Member of the South Carolina Legislature (1876), Thirty-fifth Bishop of the African Methodist Episcopal Church

Herbologist-Nutritionist
JOHN E. MOORE
New York, New York

"Herbology," says John E. Moore, "is becoming a lost art in this country. A lot of people are dying out and the knowledge is going with them." Dr. Moore, as he is often called, believes that herbs as a natural food can be a cure-all for our physical ills and an answer to survival. He also believes that eating raw foods, that is in the natural state, is more nutritious than processed foods.

The Tree of Life Bookstore sells books on herbology and plans to publish others, some of which are rare, almost forgotten works entrusted to Dr. Moore during the period of his studies. He obtained his honorary doctorate in "World Survival" from New York University's Weinstein Center for Student Living. He teaches a course "Herbs for Health and Survival" at the Tree of Life Bookstore.

Dr. Moore's interest in herbology was rooted in his birthplace of Caddogap, Arkansas, where at age 10 he studied with the Black midwives who used "tropical yam" for birth control and "red raspberry" to ease the pain of childbirth. At 15 he left his Baptist father and mother on their farm to begin his life on the road hopping trains and sleeping in cottonseed houses. This was his start as a "professional" hobo; he became a member of Hoboes of America and is the Minister of Cultural and Domestic Affairs of the Hobo International Society which has a membership of two million, of which ex-prize fighter Jack Dempsey is a member. Dr. Moore's traveling days stopped four years ago—although he still considers himself a hobo—since he considers that he is moving into "modern society" as he moves into his fifties.

For a time he worked for a small Black manufacturing firm that made over three million combs. He was the resident nutritionist until the company ceased operations. Thereafter, he held a memorable survival symposium for the Atlanta-based Institute of the Black World where he prepared an organic survival meal for 135 guests, consisting of whole wheat raisin bread with organic beets, raw corn, raw vegetable juices, nuts, teas, honey and bee pollen. He promoted organic foods as being healthier because our society puts synthetic fertilizers and poisonous chemicals in our foods, which are damaging to our health.

Even the medication from the early days in the South, he cites, were organic: eyebright for eye trouble and black walnut leaves for the purest form of iodine. He tells of how the Indians used golden seal root for skin cancer, elecampane as insulin for diabetes 2,000 years ago, and ginseng as a restorative agent for the body.

At present, Dr. Moore and his associates introduce these fascinating facts of herbology, astrology, yoga, meditation, etc., on cable TV in New York. The school was also featured on CBS-TV's "The People" in March 1976.

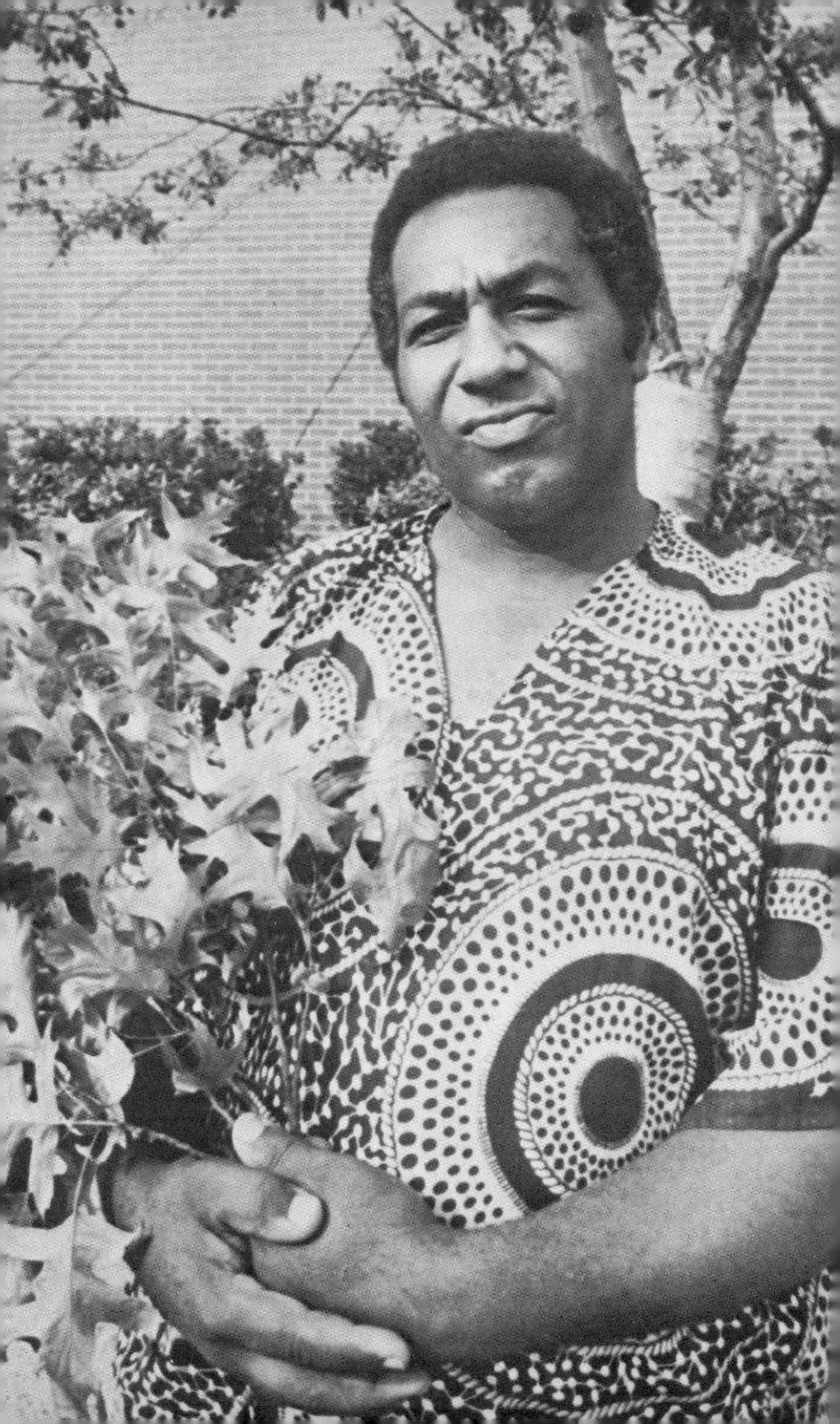

Advertising Agent
PHYLLIS REED
New York, New York

Phyllis Reed began her career in advertising after having committed herself to a lifelong ambition to be a film director and communications specialist. She started out as a film editor, working on documentaries, feature films and television commercials. Work in commercials sparked her interest in advertising, and that medium seemed the quickest way to learn film techniques. She planned to use this knowledge to become "The Lady Film Director."

"The editing room left a lot to be desired in terms of the other aspects of production," says Ms. Reed. All elements involved in film production from the conception of the idea; the actual filming that involves scripts, sets, actors; to the cutting-room table—all fascinated her. And advertising offered her the opportunity to delve into the same areas.

The business and advertising courses Phyllis Reed had taken in college plus her film background enabled her to obtain a position as assistant producer of TV commercials. Within a year she moved up to producer status at a major advertising agency. In the meantime, she set up Dalmatian Enterprises, Inc., while she was employed at the ad agency. She admits that Dalmatian really began as a film company and that due to the scarcity of resources at hand the progress of the project dissipated. To make this project work, she attempted to redirect and broaden the scope by making a decision to change the company to a total-communications service with six divisions.

Dalmatian's 100, the most visible affiliate of the company's six divisions, serves as consultant to small local businesses that connot afford larger agencies. For a nominal fee, Dalmatian's 100 advises clients on how much advertising they should have within their budget.

Although Dalmatian Enterprises services local, retail and service businesses only in New York City, both Phyllis Reed and her clients are pleased that they have achieved ad campaigns in most of the mass media in New York. She envisions broadening the scope of the company to include advertising services for national accounts, TV and documentary film production and public relations. Her working philosophy is "to do the best you can with what you have" and "to assess your position, set your objectives, plot your moves and then make those moves."

Profiles in Black

Artist
VINCENT SMITH
New York, New York

Vincent Smith was born in Brooklyn, New York. His interest in art was rooted in his pre-school days when he enjoyed tracing things—such as comic strips—on paper. During a perfectly normal childhood of ball playing, bike riding and studying the piano and saxophone, he also developed a social consciousness. He remembers his minister at the African Orthodox Church speaking about the philosophy of Marcus Garvey.

Smith quit high school to work on the Lackawanna Railroad, traveling farther North and through the South. By the time he was 17 he was well-traveled and joined the Army. The railroad and army experiences made him very aware of segregation and other injustices to Blacks, but he was not prepared to seek ways of remedying social ills at this time.

After his stint in the Army, a still professionally unfocused Smith spent two years with college students, demonstrating and distributing leaflets. That period sharpened his social and political attitudes. He read a great deal, "anything I could get my hands on, including art." From his reading he decided, "I want to be an artist."

In this discovery period Smith found that "there was practically nothing on the history of Black people in the libraries—and certainly nothing on Black astists." This absence of available information impelled Vincent Smith to create something—"something to which my people could relate." He also saw very few Black artists' works represented in galleries and museums, and the few works he saw displeased him because of their lack of relevance to the Black experience or Black movements such as the civil rights struggle and the turbulence of the Sixties. So Smith's artistic philosophy evolved: "I dedicated myself to painting a more meaningful interpretation of our ancestral as well as contemporary culture."

And so he studied art at the Art Students League and the Brooklyn Museum, both in New York, and at the Skowhegan School for Painting and Sculpture, Maine.

Vincent Smith has shown at many galleries in New York (the Larcada, Whitney Museum Art Resources Center, MUSE Children's Museum of the Brooklyn Museum), and Pennsylvania, Tennessee and Maine, and numerous galleries in Africa (Kibo Art Gallery, Kilimanjaro, Tanzania; Chemchemi Creative Arts Center, Arusha, Tanzania; Paa Ya Paa Gallery, Nairobi, Kenya). He was the illustrator of *Folklore Stories from Africa*. He has been commissioned by the New York City Board of Education to paint four murals in 1976. Currently, he is teaching at the Whitney Museum Art Resources Center in New York. Indeed, Vincent Smith is living up to his philosophy of artistic relevance to his culture as well as to the contemporary mainstream.

Profiles in Black

Music Communicator
DEE DEE McNEIL
Hollywood, California

As a pint-sized girl of six, Dee Dee McNeil announced that she wanted to be a writer. If some doubted her commitment, they have since learned to believe. In 1968, her talents of rhythm and rhyme and her ability to play piano by ear landed her a songwriters contract with Motown in Detroit.

In 1970, she drove cross country in search of new horizons with her two children perched on top of packing boxes in the back seat of the car. Arriving in Los Angeles, she joined the Watts Writers Workshop where she met the Watts Prophets, a three-man group, and toured with them on college campuses with songs and poetry. The following year, they recorded an album named after a song she wrote called "Black in a White World."

In 1972 some of her poetry was published in an anthology entitled the *Broadside Annual*. The same year, she wrote, illustrated and published a book of children's poetry called *Dee Dee Doodles*. Her work has been selected as part of *A Rock Against the Wind: Black Love Poems*, an anthology edited by Lindsay Patterson.

On the musical writing side several of her songs have been published and recorded by artists like the Four Tops, Nancy Wilson, Gladys Knight and the Pips, among others.

Dee Dee McNeil decided to pursue journalism as another writing path after writing feature articles on some of the artists she encountered. This led to freelance writing for *Black Star Magazine, Right On, Soul Teen* and other publications.

Later the recording industry beckoned and she became a publicist for A & M Records. While working for A & M, she realized the need for serving the Black press. She established the first most complete listing of the Black press at A & M Records, making it possible for many papers and publications to receive entertainment news, records for review and press passes to local performances by national recording artists.

As her reputation grew, she was offered a better position at United Artists of America which she accepted: she became the first female national press and media coordinator for the company. She met Bill Chappell at United Artists and discovered that he was attempting to build a publishing company. She became a contributing editor to his magazine, *The Soul & Jazz Record*, the first and only Black-owned and operated music trade publication in the U.S. Later she invested in his business ventures and wound up being co-publisher and associate editor.

Although she has accomplished a good deal on a high school education, she has returned to school to major in music with a minor in journalism. In addition to this, she is raising her three children and still writing both music and articles.

Profiles in Black

Public Service Television Producer
NATE LONG
Seattle, Washington

After Nate Long retired from the Air Force in 1968, he became director of SEEK (Summer Emphasis on Education and Knowledge), an experimental summer recreation program, co-sponsored by Seattle Model Cities and Seattle Public Schools. A film workshop that was part of SEEK consisted of eight youths to which a grant was given by the Seattle Model Cities Program. Later Nate Long formed Oscar Productions, Inc., a nonprofit corporation that provided on-the-job training in cinematography, still photography and television production.

Since 1970, Oscar Productions has produced a half-hour public service television series "Action: Inner-City" that is shown every week on KOMO-TV, an ABC affiliate. In 1971, Oscar Productions received the national award for outstanding achievement in training young people in photography from the Photography for Youth Foundation in New York City. This program was cited as one of the finest workshops in the country.

Hoping to produce a feature length motion picture through Oscar Productions, Nate Long went to Hollywood to learn firsthand every aspect of filmmaking. He worked on several Black films in a number of capacities, ranging from bit player to assistant director. In the spring of 1974, Oscar Productions opened the doors to the public and offered comprehensive training in TV and film production at their School of Communications.

Starting in 1972, Mr. Long served for three years as coordinator for the Black Community Arts Festivals in Seattle that featured Melvin Van Peebles, Denise Nicholas and Jim Brown as Grand Marshalls.

Mr. Long is a member of the advisory boards of the Lincoln Kilpatrick School of Acting, Los Angeles, and the Langston Hughes Community Center, Black Arts/West and Friends of Yesler Library, the last three are in Seattle. He is a member of the Independent Film Producers Association and has served on the national nominating committee for the Emmy television awards. In September 1974, Washington State University received a grant from the Department of Health, Education and Welfare to support production of a five-part television series "Black History of the Pacific Northwest." Nate Long says, "I was honored to be named project director/producer of this series."

Nate Long is married and he and his wife have one daughter.

Profiles in Black

Judge
BRUCE McM. WRIGHT
New York, New York

Bruce McM. Wright, the dynamic and forthright New York City judge who created such a furor in terms of political justice toward defendants, served for many years in the Criminal Court until his controversial transfer to the Civil Court in January 1975.

Known for his outspoken views and criticism of the criminal court system and his practice of setting low bail (for indigent defendants of minority groups who were unjustly held in prison for lack of funds for bail), Judge Wright was formally charged by the Patrolmen's Benevolent Association with having violated procedure in chastising a police officer who drew a gun on a defendant outside the courtroom, an act which he termed "a gross abuse of police power." David Ross, the citywide administrative judge, subsequently ordered Judge Wright and eight other judges to be transferred, claiming that all re-assignments were made in the best interest of the court system, and that all judges—whether of the Civil, Criminal or Family courts—must familiarize themselves with all aspects of the law.

Although Judge Wright has appealed for reinstatement to the criminal court bench, a judicial disciplinary committee in June 1975 dropped the formal charges against him although they have not resolved Judge Wright's appeal. His case is being defended by the lawyers of the Center for Constitutional Rights, the National Lawyers Guild and the National Conference of Black Lawyers.

His suit indicates a series of incidents in which police officers allegedly "showed contempt, hatred, and hostility and disrespect for Judge Wright." He names in addition to the PBA, 13 organizations and 2 district attorneys as defendants and accuses them of violating his constitutional and civil rights and of creating a "campaign of public smear against any judicial independence" and his "free speech." The last refers to the police officer episode in which Judge Wright expressed his anger and resentment.

Judge Wright's incisive speech and articulate manner were evident even in his boyhood when he recalls, "My father, an immigrant, wished me to be a medical doctor and, loyal to his middle-class ambitions, I studied the relevant sciences but at the critical moment, unable to press a scalpel into a rabbit, I decided that law was more tolerable to me." Therefore, he pursued law at Lincoln University, Pennsylvania, and after graduation, "wasted 4½ years in the First Infantry Division of the Army."

He went to Yale University Law School. Afterward he was appointed chief justice of the Court of Appeals. He spent time at what he calls, "The Wall Street Experience," concluding that financial success was not the meaning in life. "Law offered the opportunities to chase the promise of the Emancipation Proclamation and the egalitarian amendments to the Constitution."

Judge Wright and his wife have four sons. Adapting John Adams's premise that "a father studies politics and war, so that his sons might have the liberty to study mathematics and philosophy," Judge Wright thinks that "Black fathers must study racism and the struggle against it so that their sons might study the pleasures and reward of existence as human beings," rather than suffer the indignities of oppression. "The Law, no matter how much it embarrasses white America, it seems to me, is one course to humane justice. I discovered also that Blacks who press the struggle in hot pursuit of visions and revisions are often harried by society."

Surely, Judge Wright speaks these words from his own experiences.

Aircraft Supplier
L.B. JACKSON
Los Angeles, California

L. B. Jackson is a graduate of Western States College of Engineering and has an Associate of Arts degree from Harbor Junior College. After some experience in engineering sales from 1964-69, L. B. Jackson decided to go into business for himself. "When I began bidding on surplus equipment, the owner of the company became aware of my interest in branching off on my own. He was extremely discouraging and advised me to forget about it because he felt I had neither the experience nor the ability to run a successful business."

Not to be discouraged, he founded Acudata Systems Company (ASCO) in 1970, which provides the electronics industry with design engineering and the manufacturing and testing of electronic products. ASCO was established for the express purpose of developing a financially sound, community-oriented manufacturing operation in south central Los Angeles.

He states that after he encountered a tremendous amount of red tape and the usual runaround he managed to acquire some government contracts. After four years of nothing but government contracts, he finally landed some contracts with a few major aircraft companies. L. B. Jackson's plans for the future head in the direction of moving into a larger building and of handling diversified services to the aircraft industry.

Utilizing the untapped skills of the so-called hard-core unemployed, L. B. Jackson has trained individuals in engineering and manufacturing and has formed a cohesive production team. Added to his team is his son Clarence Jackson, who is a part-time buyer.

L. B. Jackson is the son of Mr. and Mrs. Shirl Jackson who are originally from Murray, Kentucky. The aircraft supplier and his wife, Jewel, reside in Carson, a suburb of Los Angeles, with their three children, Vallarie, LeDale and Clarence.

Profiles in Black

Professor Emeritus
MARJORIE HOLLOMAN PARKER
Washington, D.C.

Marjorie Holloman Parker was educated in the public schools of Washington, D.C. She obtained her Bachelor of Science degree, *magna cum laude,* from Miner Teachers College; her Master's from the University of Chicago. She created a breakthrough in the educational field when she became the first Black woman to earn a Doctor of Philosophy degree at the University of Chicago in Education. Her doctoral dissertation "Education Activities of the Freemen's Bureau" is still valuable as an educational resource in the South and federal assistance to educational and social programs.

Dr. Parker was associate professor from 1949-59 at the District of Columbia Teachers College, formerly Miner Teachers College. She was director of student teaching at Bowie State College from 1959-65. She has been guest lecturer in education at Howard University and Dumbarton College of the Holy Cross, and was visiting professor at Southern University, Baton Rouge, Louisiana.

For four summers from 1936-39, she was on the staff of the Alpha Kappa Alpha Mississippi Health Project, a prototype of free clinics and freedom schools. She became National President of the sorority in 1958, and in 1960 led a large group of Blacks on a five-nation tour of Africa. She has written two histories of the sorority.

Dr. Parker was appointed to the District of Columbia City Council from 1972-75. As councilwoman she sponsored Title 34, the Human Rights Law, protecting persons against discrimination because of race, color, religion, national origin, age, marital status, personal appearance, sexual orientation, family responsibilities, matriculation, physical handicaps, source of income or place of residence or business. She was responsible for the principle of per capita equality of funding for students enrolled in publicly supported institutions of higher learning. She was also involved in disapproval of plans to raze (old) Dunbar High School.

In 1975, Dr. Parker was appointed to the board of directors of the Industrial Bank of Washington. She has served two terms as president of Baker's Dozen, Inc. and helped to purchase and renovate a teenage center, later donated to Howard University as a field work center. She is involved in numerous other groups such as the Hospital for Sick Children, of which she is a former president and the Stoddard Baptist Home as well as other civic and community projects.

Dr. Parker is married to Judge Barrington D. Parker, of the U.S. District Court for the District of Columbia. They have two sons—Jason, a Chinese history scholar and former foreign service officer, and Barrington, Jr., an attorney practicing in New York City.

Profiles in Black

Contractor
ROOSEVELT TAYLOR
Texas City, Texas

Profiles in Black

Roosevelt Taylor, born in Harris County, Texas, has distinguished himself in the field of industrial construction. Having majored in chemistry with minors in biology and industrial education, Mr. Taylor graduated from Bishop College at Marshall, Texas, in 1956. As a self-employed construction contractor, he and his brother, Richard Taylor, began doing business as Taylor's Appliance and Lumber Company, whose primary thrust was single and multifamily housing construction.

Success, however, was not easily achieved, but fraught with struggle as the young firm overcame the vestiges of racial hostility and threats against the owners' families. With a combination of low-keyed boyish charm and Texas fortitude, Mr. Taylor in 1965 became the first Black to engage in industrial construction in the Southwest. But ever mindful of the hardship he had endured, Mr. Taylor was instrumental in opening doors for other minority firms in the area as they pursued similar lines of business in the oil refinery industry.

After five years of steady growth, the firm incorporated as La Marque United Construction Company, Inc., and expanded into general contracting. The company signed contracts with American Oil, AMOCO Chemical, Atlantic Richland, Sun Oil, Texas City Refining and other companies for such facilities as a catalyst cracker, pumping facilities and electrical load centers.

At present, the firm is housed in its own facility, which contains approximately 10,500 square feet of space. As an equal opportunity employer, the firm has a work force of 60, not including the office staff.

Mr. Taylor is also active in community affairs and is a member of the board of directors of the Houston Association of General and Sub-Contractors, and a former member of the Community Action Council of Galveston. He is married to Marie Davis of Marshall, Texas, and they have six children.

Flight Instructor
IDA VAN SMITH
Jamaica, New York

As a young girl of three, Ida Van Smith accompanied her father regularly on trips to the airport in their native town of Lumbarton, North Carolina, to watch airplanes take off and land. Fascinated, she dreamed about learning to fly, but that dream was not to materialize until years after school, marriage and four children. After high school, she attended Shaw University, Raleigh, North Carolina, where she obtained her Bachelor's in education. She then married and moved to New York City to raise a family and to teach in a public school. She also earned a Master's degree at Queens College.

Wanting additional activities to satisfy her energetic bent, she took her first flying lesson in 1967 at La Guardia Airport, later transferring to Fayetteville, North Carolina, where she noticed that some very young spectators were practically glued to the airport fence. It was then she realized the avid interest young people had in aviation and became determined to expose them to the intricacies of flying. She obtained her pilot's license a year later, flying her Cessna Skyhawk that she fondly refers to as "Babyhawk."

Back in New York, she was ready to set up flying classes for her young students and had to use the classroom in the school where she was teaching for lack of facilities. Soon other chapters were started up and all of them became known as the Ida Van Smith Flight Clubs. Besides the clubs located in Jamaica, New York, and Lumbarton, North Carolina, the one farthest away is located in St. Lucia, British West Indies. Today there are more than 300 members, ranging from elementary school to college levels, who are frequently exposed to aviation via guest speakers, trips to airports and exposure to simulators (cockpits of airplanes). She also produces and runs a program on Cable TV (Ida Van Smith Flight Club, Channel C) and teaches a course ("Introduction to Aviation") at York College, the City University of New York. She is a member of the Borough President's Committee on Aviation, The Ninety-nines (a worldwide organization of licensed women pilots founded by Amelia Earhart), the Negro Airmen International, the Alpha Kappa Alpha Sorority; the National Association of Negro and Professional Women's Clubs, among others. She was given the Key to the City of Tuskegee, Alabama. Ida Van Smith has received the Distinguished Citizens Award for contributions to society in the field of aviation for youth. She has also won the International Year of the Woman Award for "outstanding contribution to womanhood as a female pilot and flight instructor," the Coronation Ball Award for outstanding work in aviation with youth and also several loving cups and plaques from her own flight clubs.

Profiles in Black

Mrs. Smith puts together an annual journal of the clubs' activities. She also writes regular columns entitled "Come Fly With Me," "The N.Y. Voice," "Flying High in Rochdale" and "Inside Rochdale" that appear in Long Island newspapers.

Ida Van Smith has been included in the American Biographical Institute's *Community Leaders and Noteworthy Americans,* and her profile appears in *Black Americans in Aviation.*

It is time that we had become politicians, we mean, to understand the political economy and domestic policy of nations; that we had become as well as moral theorists, also the practical demonstrators of equal rights and self-government. Except we do, it is idle to talk about rights, it is mere chattering for the sake of being seen and heard—like the slave, saying something because his so-called "master" said it, and saying just what he told him to say.... (1852)

—Martin R. Delany

Newspaper Editor, Lecturer, Author, Nineteenth-century Black Nationalist Leader

Precision Products Manufacturer
JESSE J. WILLIAMS
Philadelphia, Pennsylvania

Jesse J. Williams, Jr., cannot remember when he has not known what the word "responsibility" meant. The eldest son of a family of ten from South Carolina, he worked at chores at age six from sunup to sundown. However, time was always set aside for educational purposes. Because he had a close relationship with his father, Jesse was given strong paternal encouragement to develop his full potential. He was given the opportunity to engage in advanced-electronic technology and as he developed he realized that a vacuum existed in this field as far as minorities entering the field. This realization drove him to attempt to change the situation, the basis upon which he founded the JWM Corporation, based in Philadelphia, Pennsylvania.

"Once I engaged the challenge of operating my own business," he said, "I felt it important to operate under the capitalistic system. Capitalism implies that individuals are free to work and make money where they will and they are free to compete for jobs and customers with a minimum of government restrictions."

Today JWM is among the leaders in the design, development and manufacture of high-reliability, high-volume precision products and systems. These products are used in the world's most sophisticated computers, aircraft and spacecraft systems, as well as industrial and consumer products. At the start the corporation had two engineers and six bench workers in its employ; today there 150 employees and the corporation sales are expected to exceed three million dollars.

JWM also operates a branch office in Atlanta, Georgia, which serves as headquarters to the new communications products division. The new division will service noise intercom systems and telephone interconnect systems, a multimillion-dollar market.

J.J. Williams holds a Bachelor of Science degree in chemistry from South Carolina State College. He continued graduate studies and received his Master's degree in physical chemistry and semiconductor electronics at Syracuse University and at the University of California.

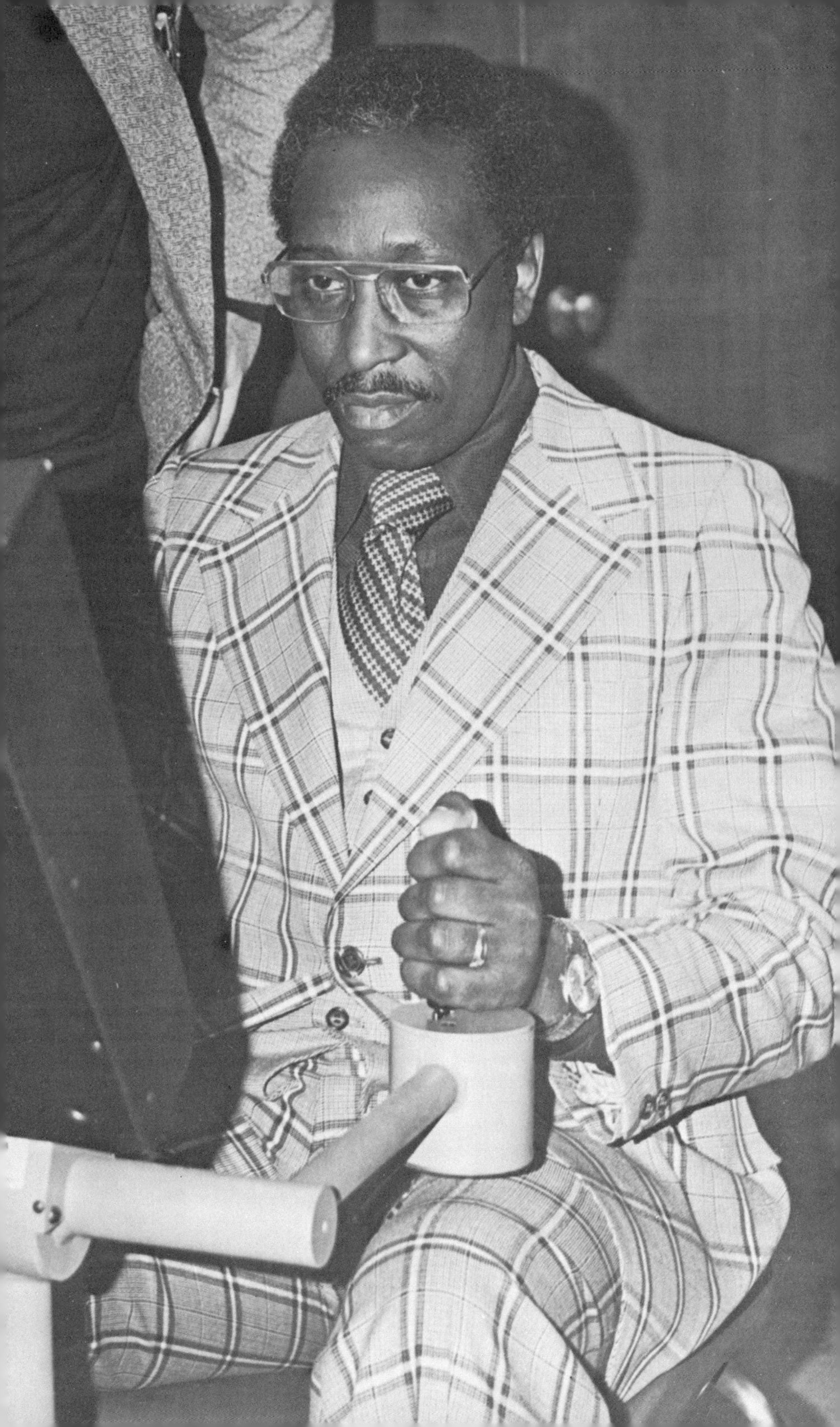

Film Producer
DANIEL A. MOORE
Atlanta, Georgia

In Dan Moore's previous career as life insurance agent, he received an award for high achievement in Philadelphia in 1960. He was ranked thirteenth in the nation for his work with Bankers Life and Casualty Insurance Company. His exposure to the community and his childhood experiences induced and reinforced his feelings that community-service programs were very necessary.

In 1961, he founded the CURE (Christians United Reaching Everyone) Community Motivation Center in Philadelphia, a group that acted as liaison between existing agencies designed to service the community and its needs. During the operation of this program and the center, it was discovered that film was a viable means of communication for instruction and motivation for the community.

The center produced several community films under Moore's direction. From this experience in 1970, he was able to form his own company called Omega Films of Philadelphia. The company grew as the needs for service of the community became more intensified.

In 1975, Dan Moore founded a second company in Atlanta, Image 7, which was designed to capture a part of the film market. His company is the only full-service Black film company in Atlanta. Moore's philosophy is this awareness of the film company's obligation to address the many pressing problems facing Black People.

Some of Moore's film credits include: "On Patrol for God," a documentary about the work of minister-policeman Melvin Floyd; "The Gang's All Here" and "Last Seen Running," about juvenile crime; "The Fourth Floor" and "The Doctor Is In," the first about nursing and the second about a Black Philadelphia physician and his research in sickle cell anemia; "Welcome Home" and "Mr. President, We Are Ready," both films about Liberia; "Bill Cosby—A Day at Graterfold," a one-hour special of Cosby's interview of inmates at the Pennsylvania prison; "Sign Here," about consumer education directed toward minority groups with warnings about signing blank contracts and making time purchases; and numerous other films.

Profiles in Black

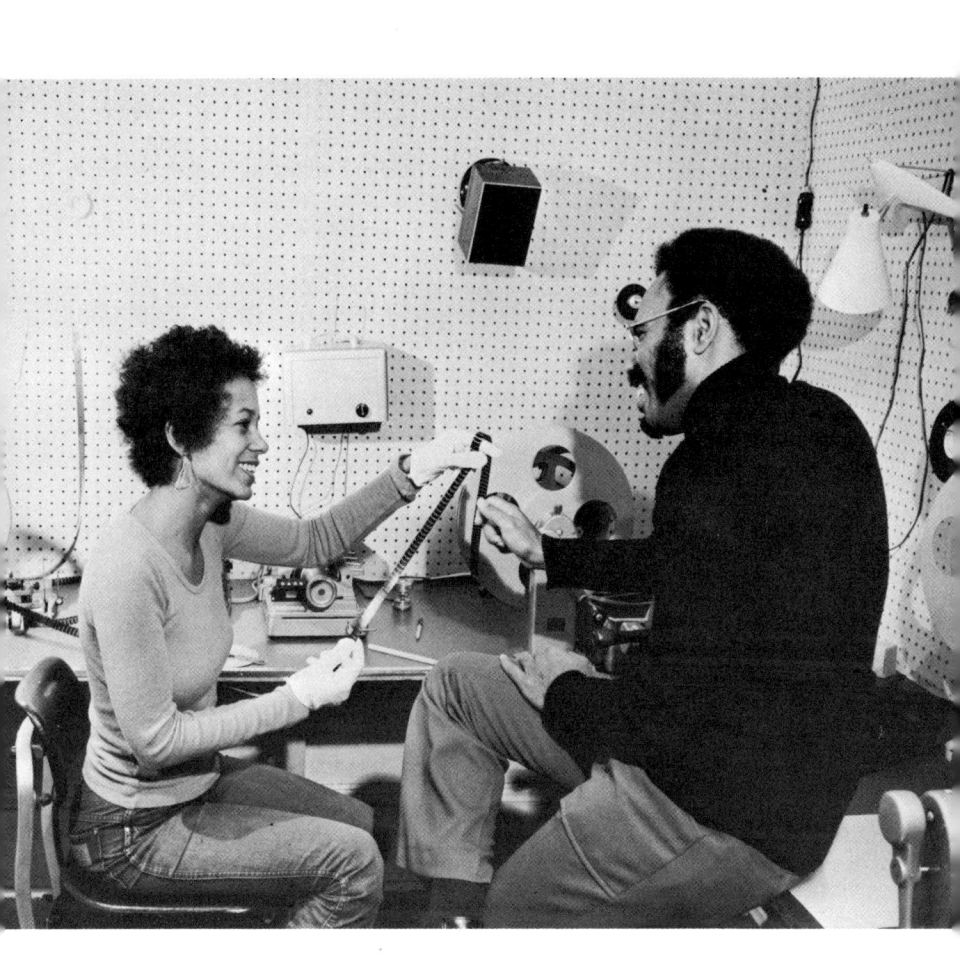

Social Gerontologist
HOBART C. JACKSON
Philadelphia, Pennsylvania

Hobart C. Jackson serves on numerous committees and participates in conferences, workshops and seminars as a speaker, discussion leader, consultant and resource person in the field of aging, or gerontology. He has presented papers and contributed at conferences of the American Association of Homes for the Aging, National Conference on Social Welfare, National Health Council, National Council on the Aging, the National Caucus on the Black Aged, the Gerontological Society, Annual Conference on Aging at the University of Michigan and the White House Conference on Aging, among many others. He has received about 40 awards for his achievements from national, state and local organizations.

He was administrator of the Stephen Smith Geriatric Center from 1949-74. He is now the executive vice president of the organization. During his administration the occupancy of the Center increased from 45 to 350 residents and tenants, and the staff grew from 19 to 150. Over one million dollars in improvements were made to the old buildings. The Center's annual budget is 20 times what it was in 1949. A new infirmary was completed in 1961 which added 50 beds for the handicapped, disabled and chronically ill. Most of the funds were secured during Mr. Jackson's administration.

Of great significance has been Hobart Jackson's volunteer work as a founder and the first president of The National Caucus on the Black Aged. The Caucus was organized in a year prior to the 1971 White House Conference on Aging to give visibility to the special unfortunate plight of the Black elderly. One of its projects was the establishment of the National Center on the Black Aged in Washington, D.C. The Center does research, disseminates information, supports existing and beginning services and other programs in behalf of older Black Americans.

Mr. Jackson was on the executive committee of the White House Conference. Currently, he serves as the chairman of an advisory council that is part of the United States Senate Special Committee on Aging.

A *cum laude* graduate of Morehouse College, Atlanta, Georgia, he also holds a Master's degree in social service from the Bryn Mawr College Graduate Department of Social Work and Social Research, Pennsylvania, where he is now a lecturer in gerontology. He has also taken special courses in gerontology and administration at Temple University and the University of Pennsylvania School of Social Work. He is a fellow of the Gerontological Society and a member of both the Academy of Certified Social Workers and the National Association of Social Workers. He is also a licensed nursing-home administrator.

He has served on commissions or task forces under three presidents, four governors and four mayors.

Profiles in Black

Mr. Jackson is married to the former Elaine Bethel, a supervisor with the Philadelphia Department of Public Welfare. They have three children—Hobart, Jr., Dale and Marlene.

Pediatrician
DORIS LOUISE WETHERS
New York, New York

Doris Wethers did her undergraduate work at Queens College, New York City, and received her Doctor of Medicine degree from Yale University School of Medicine. Her father was a physician who strongly supported her choice of medicine as a career. She served as a rotating intern until 1953 when she began her training in pediatrics. She was appointed in 1965 as director of pediatrics at Knickerbocker Hospital in New York City and served in this capacity until July 1973. In 1969, she accepted a second directorship at Sydenham Hospital, also in New York City. Although she is interested in all aspects of health and welfare of children, she has concentrated on sickle cell anemia, a disease that is prevalent among and hereditary to Blacks.

Dr. Wethers has done clinical studies and has lectured extensively to the public about all aspects of sickle cell disease. She has organized three clinics that service patients with this blood disorder which is a form of hemoglobinopathy. She has served as consultant to the government and to private organizations to aid them in the counseling, diagnosing and treating of sickle cell anemia, both in the States and in foreign countries, including the Bahamas and several of the independent African nations.

She has written medical tracts about setting up programs for screening and detecting this blood disorder. In addition to her writing and editing of works on S-hemoglobinopathy, she has aided in setting up screening programs in New York City. She is currently doing a ten-year retrospective study on pediatric cases of sickle cell disease for two New York City hospitals—Sydenham and St. Luke's Hospital Center.

Dr. Wethers has been instrumental in setting up parent groups for parents of children with sickle cell disease.

Since 1957, Dr. Wethers has been on the pediatric faculty of Columbia University College of Physicians & Surgeons. She is currently associate professor of clinical pediatrics. In 1974, following her resignation from Sydenham, she accepted the appointment of director of the Department of Pediatrics at St. Luke's Hospital Center, a pediatric training program that is affiliated with the Columbia University College of Physicians & Surgeons.

Profiles in Black

Labor Mediator
HEZEKIAH BROWN
New York, New York

Hezekiah Brown, one of ten children, born in Mobile, Alabama, left home at an early age. He traveled to Virginia, Florida and New York, where he joined his sister Theresa in Buffalo. His first job in Buffalo was at the Veterans Hospital in the Dietetic Department where he served food for approximately three months and later drove trucks for General Motors for four months in 1956. Following his military obligation (1956-58), he returned to work at General Motors in 1959 and married Christine Harper the following year.

In 1963, he was elected to his first position with the United Auto Workers local 1173. He served two terms as alternate committeeman and later was elected district shop committeeman. Mr. Brown realized the intensity and seriousness of his dealing with people and regretted having stopped his education before finishing high school. He went back to school to obtain his high school diploma and later enrolled at Cooperate Community College, attending four nights a week, four hours a night while holding a full-time job. In the same period he was elected to the executive board of the UAW. Mr. Brown saw the need to further his education in both academic and collective bargaining areas. He attended the UAW School of Collective Bargaining at Alfred State University, Labor Management College at the Diocese of Buffalo and the UAW Arbitrator School.

In May 1971, he was elected president of UAW local 1173 that represents 3,500 members. At 32, he has the distinction of being the youngest president to serve in this capacity. Mr. Brown was well on his way within the UAW structure when he changed course and decided he wanted to become a federal mediator. He began his career as Commissioner of the Federal Mediation and Conciliation Service in October 1972 with a government service rating of 12, and has now been promoted to GS 14. He is the tenth Black in the U.S. to serve in this capacity.

Most recently he was involved in mediation between several New York newspapers and the newspaper guild; United Parcel Service and the Teamsters; the University of Bridgeport and the American Association of University Professors, as well as several hospitals.

He is a member of the Society of Professionals in Dispute Resolutions (SPIDR) and Industrial Relations Research Association (IRRA). In 1974, he was the recipient of the Black Achievers in Industry Award, and in 1975, he appeared in *Who's Who in Labor.*

Profiles in Black

Equal Employment Administrator
WILLIAM LAYTON
Washington, D.C.

William W. Layton was born at the Virginia Manual Training School where his father was an instructor and later superintendent of the correctional institution. He attended high school in Richmond, Virginia, where he was known as the Black Poet Laureate. In 1933, he helped to organize a young people's boycott of a chain food store in Richmond that refused to hire Blacks except in janitorial capacities. He attended Lincoln University, Pennsylvania, and did his graduate studies in social science at Fisk University, Nashville, Tennessee.

After his studies he served on the American Youth Commission as a field interviewer in the late Thirties. This commission published the first comprehensive series on the plight of Black youth in the United States.

In 1939, William Layton was an attendance officer in the Nashville public schools where he introduced innovative methods of treating truancy problems relating to poverty in the Black community.

Five years later he became the industrial relations director of the Columbus (Ohio) Urban League where he placed hundreds of Blacks who had migrated to the city during World War II in previously all-white industries. He became director of the Greater Muskegon (Michigan) Urban League in 1951 and organized an employment program that immeasurably improved the economics of the community. In 1959, he became the first director of the Lansing Region of the Michigan Fair Employment Practices Commission which aided in the monetary settlement to a complainant in the case of *Jimmerson vs. The Savoy Theatre*. He organized and directed the Equal Employment Office Contract Compliance staff of the Department of Agriculture in Washington, D.C., in 1965. He initiated compliance actions which improved the hiring situation of Blacks, especially in the South where various firms held federal contracts. He became the first director of the EEO in 1971 for the Board of Governors of the Federal Reserve System.

As a hobby, William Layton collects documents from the Abolitionist Movement and the Civil War period. His collection includes items related to John Brown, George Washington Carver, Charles Sumner, Harriet Beecher Stowe and others. Mr. Layton's ancestry can be traced to 1737 from documents in his collection.

Profiles in Black

Dean and Professor of Dentistry
JEANNE CRAIG SINKFORD
Washington, D.C.

"You certainly don't look like a dentist!" many people tell Dr. Jeanne Sinkford upon first meeting her.

She replies that dentistry is a perfect career for women because of their sense of esthetics and beauty, their ability to be sympathetic and their small hands which help them work in delicate areas such as the mouth. Dr. Sinkford recommends dentistry as a career for young women "without reservation because it affords a very useful, purposeful existence."

It was when she was a junior in college that Jeanne Sinkford decided that she wanted to go to dental school, and her family dentist encouraged her. This kind of encouragement is rare among Black professionals, so Jeanne Sinkford was very fortunate to have her parents and an understanding adult to support her career dreams.

Although her family was not financially well off, all four daughters were encouraged to obtain as much education as possible so they worked out a "family plan," whereby the older would help the next in line upon finishing college. However, young Jeanne's education took eight years and her younger sister wound up helping *her* instead, even though there were scholarships and summer jobs to lighten the financial load. Jeanne Sinkford graduated first in her dental class at Howard University in 1958.

She taught prosthodontics (a branch of teeth work involving crowns and bridgework) for two years before obtaining her Master's (1962) and Doctor of Philosophy (1963) degrees at Northwestern University. She became head of the Prosthodontics Department in 1964-68–a first for women in the U.S. dental schools. In 1975, Dr. Sinkford became the first woman dental school dean in the U.S. Before becoming Dean, she served as Associate Dean and Research Coordinator at the same time.

In her teaching she advises her students not to let financial obstacles stand in the way of a dental education and that one does not have to be an Einstein if one is able to handle a college education. She also counsels, "It's important to know what you like to do because a career should not simply be work, but should be enjoyable, challenging and rewarding."

Besides teaching, practice and research, she has written many articles on prosthodontics and has served on the Council of Dental Education of the American Prosthodontic Society, the American Pedodontic Society, the International Association for Dental Research, the American Association for the Advancement of Science. She is the recipient of numerous awards and fellowships, such as the Alumni achievment awards from Northwestern and Howard universities and a Fellowship of the American and the International College of Dentists. She is also active in Jack and Jill of America.

Dr. Sinkford is married to a pediatrician and they have three children.

Profiles in Black

Dry Cleaning Entrepreneur
BERKELEY BURRELL
Washington, D.C.

"I decided I was never going to work for anyone else. I was tired of answering whistles and bells and decided to be my own boss. I opened a dry-cleaning shop in downtown Washington and contracted the cleaning work out," so said Dr. Berkeley G. Burrell. He then became a leading Black entrepreneur as well as president of the National Business League, a position he has held since 1962.

Profiles in Black

Berkeley Burrell was born in Washington, D.C., in 1919, where he attended public schools and Howard University as a political science major. Financial problems caused the young Burrell to drop out of college but did not diminish his desire to succeed.

After World War II, Burrell, with $100 in hand, decided rather than return to his pre-war job of driving a cab that he would find more room for success and growth in the dry-cleaning business. He hired his girl friend to work for him at $25 a week. Recounting the story with a smile, Burrell said he figured that if he married her, she wouldn't cost him anything. So he did and his wife, Parthenia, made the transition a serious joint venture and is still his business partner.

By 1951, Burrell's Superb Cleaners had expanded to five shops, but the young entrepreneur was recalled to active service during the Korean conflict and closed all but one of his shops. That one his wife operated in his absence. After leaving the service, he expanded again by purchasing the cleaning plant that had serviced his shops. Today Burrell's Superb Cleaners operates out of a central plant serving several outlets, two of which are owned by Dr. Burrell's dry-cleaning company.

As president of the National Business League, Dr. Burrell is helping to strengthen the 163,000 Black-owned businesses in America. He is also president of the Booker T. Washington Foundation.

Presidential recognition of Dr. Burrell's ability has resulted in his appointment to the National Commission on Productivity, the National Business Council for Consumer Affairs, the National Minority Purchasing Council and the vice chairmanship of the President's Advisory Council for Minority Enterprise.

Dr. Burrell was awarded a Doctor of Arts degree from Virginia College in Lynchburg, Virginia. His participation in civic organizations includes membership on the board of directors of the Robert Russa Moton Foundation and Corporation for Blacks in Public Broadcasting, among others. In the educational arena, he is chairman of the Board of Regents of Daniel Hale Williams University, the innovative collegiate institution.

Businessman, philanthropist, lecturer, author of *Getting It Together: Black Businessmen in America* and syndicated news column *Down to Business*, presidential appointee, husband and father of one son—Berkeley, Jr.—the senior Burrell has "made it" in spite of obstacles and continues to work toward even greater contributions to Black economic growth. He says optimistically, "It is unfortunate that historically, we haven't had the money, time or people to do what is needed to be done to make Black business a stronger economic force in the nation. Today we stand closer to achieving that objective than ever before."

Travel Consultant
BARBARA GILLIAM
New York, New York

Barbara Gilliam was born in New York City. She studied at City College in 1954 and studied French at the Alliance Francaise in New York City. Travel became an important element in her life when she began her childhood visits to relatives in Virginia and North Carolina by bus and by train. She especially developed a taste for travel by boat from her memories of crossings on the old Cape Charles Ferry. The subsequent trips to Puerto Rico, Bermuda and then Europe attracted her into the travel business, although after graduation from high school she had a number of clerical jobs and a job in sales promotion with the cosmetic company Alexandra de Markoff, a subsidiary of Charles of the Ritz.

Her ten-year career in the travel business began as a trainee with the wholesale/retail travel agency where she dealt with student travel, the "Summer Sessions Abroad" programs, the Mediterranean holiday cruises and customized tours. She is currently the manager of special markets for EGR Travel International, Inc., a position that affords her the time to escort travel groups and to develop programs. She has since broadened her own travel experiences in Western Europe, Africa, the Middle East, South and Central Americas and the Polynesian Islands.

She claims that the traveling industry is an expanding field that is constantly inproving, and that it is a profession open to Black men and women. Women, however, might be more attracted to the field, she thinks, because of the public contact involved, although at the beginning the salary is not high paying. This drawback exists possibly because the original travel bureaus were "mom and pop" operations that did not require unionization of employees, a status that has not much changed. However, the administrative jobs in travel are better paying.

To learn about travel management and other aspects of the travel field, a person can enroll at a number of universities that offer such courses. There are specialized schools geared to teaching about travel (see Sources at the back of this book). Airlines frequently hold classes in making out tickets, etc.

Ms. Gilliam finds her particular job challenging in creating a desire for travel in people. In the future she would like to write articles about travel which would be informative to Blacks.

This well-rounded travel agent has two avocations: tennis—in which she played actively with the American Tennis Association Circuit—and opera—managing the Opera Buffa in New York in 1972, and helping the company to obtain support from the Borough President of Manhattan Musicians Fund and the New York State Council on the Arts.

Profiles in Black

The important lesson we should learn, and be able to teach, is how to make every gift, whether gold or talent, fortune or genius, subserve the cause of crushed humanity and carry out the greatest idea of the present age, the glorious idea of human brotherhood. (1859)

—Frances Ellen Watkins Harper

Poet, Lecturer

Professor, Administrator
EDWARD MAPP
New York, New York

Edward Mapp grew up in Harlem. Of his early background he says, "From my earliest days as a youth I had profound respect for the communication arts. My library card was a passport to a world of wonderful possibilities." When he won an essay contest on Brotherhood at the YMCA at 13 he realized that it was his first formal role of being a communicator.

He worked part time as a messenger through high school and full time as a clerk while taking night courses at the City College of New York. He obtained a Bachelor of Arts degree in 1953 and a Master's degree in library science from Columbia University. He then earned a Doctor of Philosophy in mass communications from New York University.

Dr. Mapp's intense interest in film communications led him to his writing about Black actors in the medium, a work entitled *Blacks in American Films.*

He was on the faculty of Alexander Hamilton High School and on staff of the New York Public Library when he was invited to join the faculty of the City University of New York in 1964. In addition to his administrative duties, he serves as professor of the library sciences department and has been appointed chairman of the library department of New York City Community College.

In 1974, he was appointed to the Advisory Committee of the National Project Center for Film and the Humanities. The committee serves as consultative body to the Project Director. The federally funded Project Center designs programs for general adult public concerns, using a combination of film and written materials to broaden public access to the humanities so that the humanities can be applied to contemporary issues.

Dr. Mapp has written articles for professional journals as well as several books (*Puerto Rican Perspectives* and *A Directory of Blacks in the Performing Arts*, the latter to be published in 1976). He has received the 1970 Founders Day Award from New York University for outstanding work as a scholar. He has been praised as an outstanding scholar, administrator and humanist and has been cited for his knowledge of film. Dr. Mapp is a member of 100 Black Men and is on the Board of Directors of the United Nations Association. He was also interviewed on tape for the collection at the Schomburg Center for Research in Black Culture.

According to the Project Director, Dr. Mereld D. Keys, Dr. Mapp's achievements in the academic world and his knowledge of minority-group relations will be of invaluable aid to the Project Center.

Dr. Mapp believes that "media is the key to all that I have been, am now and will be in the advancement of myself, my family and my race."

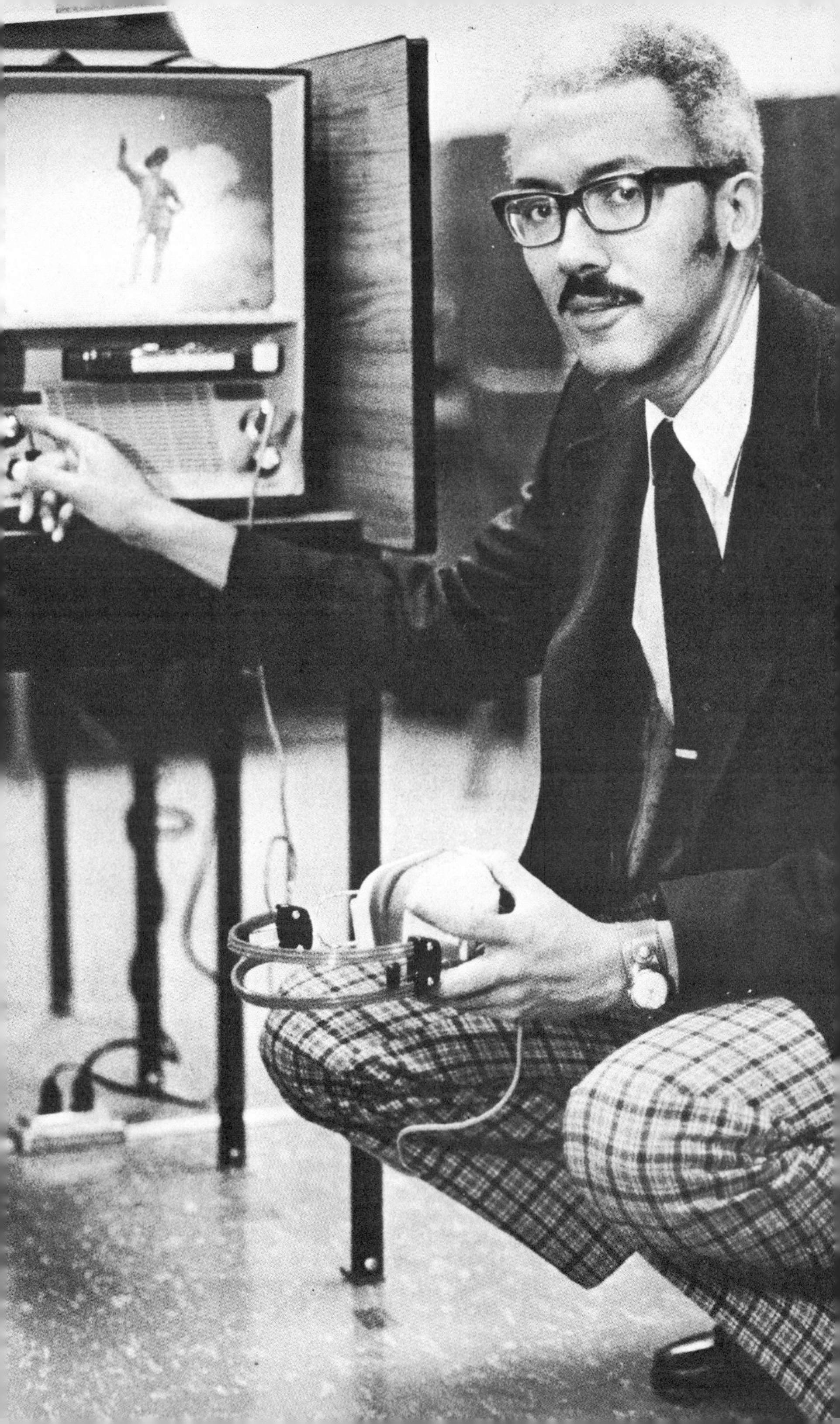

Bank President
CHARLES M. REYNOLDS, JR.
Norfolk, Virginia

"My personal philosophy is to exemplify at all times a conscientious effort to upgrade the development of minority businesses in order to provide sound lending practices of extending credit to minorities who heretofore have been unable to borrow monies at financial institutions. Also to make a contribution in the area of civic and economic endeavors in the community where I live. As a president of a minority institution, I'm allowed a unique advantage both to render a service to the community and provide an uplift to the residents who never had the opportunity to enjoy some of the financial rewards that a bank offers to its constituents. This work is a wonderful experience and I enjoy it."

Thus begins the solid philosophy of Charles M. Reynolds, Jr., president of The Atlantic National Bank of Norfolk, Virginia. Mr. Reynolds began his banking career in 1966 as the first Black appointed to the position of assistant national bank examiner in the region which covers Georgia, Florida and South Carolina. Three years later he became the first Black national bank examiner of that same region. In February 1971, Mr. Reynolds joined Citizens Trust Bank in Atlanta, Georgia, in the capacity of executive vice president and was elected president three months later.

"I had a personal reason for accepting the tough job as Citizens Trust Bank president; I was less surprised at management practices at the bank than the public, that it was no different from white institutions that started operating out of their hip pocket a hundred years ago. One man, one control for almost fifty years, so I had to initiate some changes in my four years' tenure."

What Mr. Reynolds did was to institute an annual CPA audit, form the first major Black holding company in the state, upgrade managerial control, formulate a pension plan and bylaws, establish a public relations program from which was derived a new bank logo—or emblem—institute written lending policies and establish a second branch of the bank. Having done all he could do for Citizens Trust, he resigned at the end of 1974. At the beginning of 1975, he accepted the presidency of Atlantic National Bank in Norfolk, going into his job with gusto and with the reputation of a man who works at turning dreams into gospel.

Charles Reynolds is a native of Thomasville, Georgia. He obtained his undergraduate degree from Morehouse College, Atlanta, in 1961, and studied at Wayne State University, Detroit, Michigan; Atlanta University, Georgia; and Columbia University, New York City. He taught at Southside Junior High School, Albany, Georgia, and was the chairman of the social studies department before embarking on his banking career.

Mr. Reynolds is married, and he and his wife have two sons.

Profiles in Black

Social Service Director
ANNIE ESTELLE MALONE
New York, New York

Annie Estelle Malone, born on a Virginia farm, grew up in her grandparents' large household. After graduating from high school, she moved to New York City to live with her mother. She wanted to enter college, but could not until she had made up the courses she lacked. It was in her new environment that she first became aware that her family was poor.

Annie Malone did not give up pursuit of studying in college. After serving in the Air Force for nearly four years, she returned to New York City to obtain a Bachelor of Arts degree from Hunter College and a Master's in Social Work from Columbia University. In the meantime Miss Malone continued her affiliation with the military in an active Reserves program. In April 1976, she was promoted to the rank of major, an honor for Black women who are in administrative positions. She is also active with the 369th Veterans' Association and is the editor of its bimonthly newspaper.

For the past eight years, Miss Malone has been the director of social services at St. Barnabas House, a social service agency that is part of the Episcopal Mission Society. She has assisted in the development of several programs for SBH. She has helped in the establishment of St. Peter's School, a general institution for children in Peekskill, New York, and has aided in the development of group homes for children, and has researched the Parent Therapist Program, a novel idea in child welfare. In June 1972, students who were pursuing a Bachelor of Social Work degree from the New York Training Institute, Adelphi University, were assigned to St. Barnabas House under her supervision for field-work training. She has also added students from the Master's of Social Work program.

Annie Malone says her interests vary from traveling to religion, to the military to social work. "Some people may think that there is a contradiction in my personal philosophy because of the variety of interests, but that is only an assumption on their part. I find this diversified background has helped me to develop personally and has readied me for the present pursuit—a Doctor of Social Welfare degree."

Miss Malone is an active member of the Transfiguration Lutheran Church in Manhattan and is also president of the board of trustees of the church. She has traveled extensively to Jamaica, Puerto Rico, Haiti, seven countries in Africa, Hong Kong, Japan, Mexico and Canada.

Miss Malone feels the factor responsible for her success is her religious training and her positive image of Black identity. She counsels people to "know your own capabilities." She thinks that "Blacks should not get caught up in the slavery period; slavery is only a detour in the long road of our history." She recommends that Blacks should concentrate on their heritage and should realize that "You are somebody."

Profiles in Black

Funeral Service Director
JOHN ALLEN CHILDS III
Redbank, New Jersey

When John Allen Childs graduated from Redbank Regional High School, although he was not aware of the processes of learning he would have to undergo, he knew that he wanted to go into funeral service work. His uncle in Nashville, Tennessee, owned a funeral home, and a cousin in Philadelphia, Pennsylvania, worked in a morgue. His grandmother had unfulfilled aspirations to be a funeral director. His mother, who was supportive of his desired career, took him for an interview at the James H. Hunt Funeral Home in Asbury Park, New Jersey. The upshot of the talk was that Childs was given a three-month period to "look-see," during which he gained experiences in all aspects of mortuary procedures.

While working at the Hunt funeral home as a director, he registered with the State Board of Mortuary Sciences as a registered apprentice in September 1960. For over a year he studied at the American Academy Macalester Institute of Funeral Services. Childs took the national and state board exams for a license, tests that are divided into written and practical. The practical part of the test takes place in a predesignated funeral home where the examinee may be asked to do an arrangement or an embalment that could cover questions pertaining to the human anatomy or to work out a blood tracing. For a brief period in 1965, he worked at Wigham Funeral Home in Newark, at the time the largest Black funeral home in New Jersey, and at the Cottons Funeral Home in Newark and Orange. Although he learned a great deal at Wigham in a more professional atmosphere, he felt that due to the largeness of the home that the service was not as personalized as at Hunt's. He thought that his work experience at Hunt's contributed to a major portion of his working knowledge.

In 1968, Childs's father, a glazier, offered financial aid so that Childs could set up his own funeral home. When Childs attempted to set up his own business he encountered tremendous difficulty in securing loans from banks. He received partial loans from friends, eventually gaining a seller-held mortgage and business-improvement loans from banks. His staff worked on a per diem basis and gradually his business has improved over the years.

At present he is about to open up another funeral home in Lakewood, New Jersey, in collaboration with his former employer and mentor, James H. Hunt.

Profiles in Black

Construction Company Owner
WILLIAM T. SYPHAX
Arlington, Virginia

William T. Syphax was born in Arlington, Virginia. He did his undergraduate work at Virginia State College and received his Master's degree in engineering from George Washington University in 1964. He began his career with the Department of Defense in 1943. He left in 1964 with the status of the chief of advanced-memory devices with a government civil service rating of GS15. He served with the Air Force in World War II as an officer.

Mr. Syphax, at 55, is the founder of the first Black construction company in northern Virginia. This enterprise, based in Arlington, has been successful in contracting over eight million dollars in business for housing and offices. He likes to recount his beginnings as a youth on campus at Virginia State in 1938 when all he had was $70 and a pawnshop suit and had to work his way through four years to obtain a degree in mathematics.

He claims that doing business in Washington, D.C., has it drawbacks, namely, his company has had to rely more frequently on Black subcontractors who were denied loans, bonding or other backing which white subcontractors have been able to secure. Blacks have not been known to establish subcontracting firms in the Virginia suburbs. They receive aid in the form of bookkeeping or administrative aid, but what Syphax feels is really needed is equity or venture capital that doesn't have to be paid back immediately like Small Business Administration loans do. He claims that his business objective is not just to make money but to set an example of success for Black youngsters. His wife, Margarite, one of two Black female certified property managers in the country, plays an important role in the firm.

He became director of the Virginia State College Board of Visitors, and aided the school to obtain a grant from the National Science Foundation, Washington, D.C., that will provide funds to support appointments of minority graduate students for three-year periods which began in 1974.

Profiles in Black

Business School Operator
JESSIE MENIFIELD RATTLEY
Newport News, Virginia

Jessie Menifield Rattley was born and raised in Birmingham, Alabama. Upon completion of high school in 1947, she entered Hampton Institute where she worked her way through college. She earned a B.S. degree in business education and secretarial science with honors in 1951. She has taken graduate courses at Hampton Institute, IBM Data Processing and LaSalle Extension University.

After graduation from Hampton Institute, Mrs. Rattley established the business department of Huntington High School—the first Black high school in Newport News to offer business training. Mrs. Rattley founded the Peninsula Business College. On June 9, 1952, as owner-operator-professor, she officially opened the doors for 15 students.

In 1970, Mrs. Rattley was the first Black and first woman to be elected to the Newport News City Council. She was top vote-getter in the 1974 election for councilwoman, re-elected to a four-year term. In 1972, she was elected first vice chairwoman of the state Democratic party. She is a member of the National Democratic Committee, serving on the credentials committee and the by-laws committee.

In 1974, she was elected second vice chairwoman of the National Black Caucus of Local Elected Officials. Mayor Tom Bradley appointed her vice chairwoman of the Effective Government Policy committee that same year.

Mrs. Rattley was the first Black elected to the Virginia Municipal League Executive Committee in 1974 and she serves on the legislative committee and the employee-management relations committee. She was appointed by the governor to serve on the Criminal Justice and Crime Prevention Task Force for Volunteerism and also as a member of a special task force to study Virginia jails.

In March 1975, she was elected treasurer of the Democratic State Chairmen Association. A month later she was appointed to assist the department of education and mental health and mental retardation in a study regarding provision of appropriate training and education to children in state institutions.

Profiles in Black

Architect, Urban Planner
WENDELL J. CAMPBELL
Chicago, Illinois

Wendell J. Campbell was born and raised in East Chicago, Illinois. Upon graduation from high school in 1945, Campbell was immediately drafted into the Army and discharged 14 months later with the rank of battalion sergeant major. His interest in community affairs began in 1947 when he helped to end discrimination in the local theatres through his legal suits and leadership of the East Chicago youth councils.

Mr. Campbell attended Indiana University and later Illinois Institute of Technology where he majored in architecture and minored in city planning. He received his Bachelor of Architecture degree in 1956.

Since 1950, he has worked for several architectural firms in and around the Chicago area, specializing in all phases of commercial and residential design. In 1956, he accepted a position at the Purdue-Calumet Development Foundation in East Chicago, Illinois, as an architect-planner and assisted in the preparation of urban renewal plans for the area in which he was raised. During the following ten years he worked in all facets of urban renewal from project planning to project execution.

Wendell Campbell was concerned with the frustration of tenants being displaced and with the lack of imagination and consideration toward these persons by many prospective developers in their planning. He resigned from urban renewal in 1966 and organized the firm of Wendell Campbell Associates, Inc., Architects and Urban Planners. One of his first jobs was a position as urban-design consultant to his former employer in the planning and administration of projects.

The firm was instrumental in organizing and serving as technical consultants to grass-roots organizations that were primarily interested in participating in urban renewal and development of their own communities. The firm was expanded to include all phases of architectural work and has since participated in the design development of neighborhood facilities centers, public housing (both turnkey and conventional), multifamily government-assisted programs, public schools, institutional buildings and consulting services for model agencies.

Mr. Campbell is a member of the American Institute of Architects and the National Organization of Minority Architects. He holds a certificate from the National Council of Architectural Registration Boards and is the 1976 recipient of the AIA Medal, awarded in memory of Whitney M. Young, Jr., in recognition of assuming professional responsibility for some of the more pressing social issues of today.

Profiles in Black

Women's Newspaper Editor
MARIE WRIGHT TEASLEY
Detroit, Michigan

Marie Wright Teasley is the daughter of the late George Hannibal Wright, who was editor and publisher of the *Hannibal Register,* a weekly newspaper published in Hannibal, Missouri. As a child, Marie spent much time in the print shop of the paper that undoubtedly bore a strong influence in shaping her career in communications and media. Her mother was a seamstress, an occupation which might have influenced Marie's choice as Women's Editor.

When her family moved to Detroit in 1948 she wrote a weekly column for a northwest Detroit newspaper. Her interest in journalism was held in abeyance at Northwestern High School when she was published only once although she was on the staff of the paper. At Wayne State University she wrote a regular column for the *Wayne Collegian* and for the *Pittsburgh Courier* as well as doing student promotion work and correspondence for the Philip Morris Company in New York. It was at this point she decided on journalism as a career. In her third year she dropped out to marry Ron Teasley, WSU's top athlete who is now the award-winning basketball and baseball coach at Northwestern High School, and they have two sons and a daughter.

In between her career as wife and mother, she kept up journalism assignments as well as odd jobs as a seamstress. The latter job included making caps and uniforms for Standard Oil Company. Drawing upon these experiences in her journalistic career, she joined the *Chronicle* staff in 1966 and was appointed Women's Editor in 1972 by Editor-Publisher Longworth Quinn. She is concerned not only with fashion, but she also concentrates on the inner Black woman and researches and discusses issues like dating, marriage, women's lib and abortion. The response to her advice has been overwhelming because of the relevant manner in which she puts the subject matter to her readers. As for her own ability, she explains, "I'm young enough to relate to the younger Black woman because I believe her commitment to the higher ideals of Black womanhood is firm, yet old enough to understand the viewpoint of the pioneer Black woman." Added to that fortunate situation are her open mind and positive attitude which help to bridge the two elements.

For her work she has been awarded the 1975 NNPA (National Newspaper Publishers Association) for Best Women's Pages; 1974 Best Supplement NNPA; 1974 Detroit Catholic Diocese Woman of the Year; 1974-75 National Media Woman of the Year; Ida B. Wells Award, New Orleans; 1974-75 Detroit Media Woman of the Year plus numerous other citations.

Marie Wright Teasley's two joys in life are watching her sons go on to law school—one of whom is a graduate of Northwestern University and the other is a Wayne State grad—and her daughter grow up and realizing the privilege and pleasure of working in Detroit which she feels is a cosmopolitan and exciting city.

Profiles in Black

Correction Officer
CHARLES R. TONIC
New York, New York

After serving six years of an 11-16-year sentence for armed robbery and then released from Leesburg Institution, New Jersey, Charles Tonic was ready to "take his place in society." Although prison officials had not offered him any rehabilitation program, he discovered in prison that the first few months of the "shock of incarceration" will determine what an inmate becomes and his future in the outside world upon release. A prisoner might lie around doing nothing or he might program himself to be productive. Tonic says, "I was released from incarceration with [a] highly developed sense of motivation. My desire, as it continues today, was to be as valuable an aid to positive change in the criminal justice system as possible. My direction was to work within the community, preaching if you will, the message 'Don't forget the prisons.' "

Tonic feels that community people care very little about what goes on in prisons, as long as the "animals" are kept away from the community. And that is the logic and motivation behind his post-prison career, Project REHAB, in New York City, a therapeutic and motivational counseling program for former inmates. He is currently director of this project.

His post-prison career began with aid from a sympathetic parole officer. When Tonic applied for an administrative job at the U.S. Census Bureau, he was not hired because "I was an ex-inmate who had only been out of the institution for three and one-half years and not the required five years. Instead I was offered a token clerk position."

When he later applied to Project Vista he was unable to satisfy academic requirements for the job and was denied employment. However, he was able to get on a task force with the Department of Correction to study conditions in New York City's detention institutions, acting as liaison between inmates and the task force, doing dietetic, medical, social service, administrative and budgetary analysis. Later he worked in the public relations department. He set up an executive reporting system, whereby different departments gave daily reports, and a monitor system to regulate the flow of 3,500 people involved in various community programs. He is currently management analyst of the Riker's Island mental health center, doing in-depth analysis of problems in institutions.

Born in Passaic, New Jersey, the oldest of four brothers and one sister, Tonic lived the life of a loner, separated from his peers because he had defective vision, and sheltered in a quiet residential world. Always the youngest and smallest in his outside environment, he got away from the sphere of family influence when he was "busted." After high school, he worked for a while but quit his job and just hung out. When he fell under the influence of the Street his activities led him to prison. He took numerous courses in criminal law while in prison and after his release he earned a Bachelor of Science degree in criminal justice at Empire State College.

Profiles in Black

Through Project REHAB, he hopes to educate former inmates in being better able to relate to their own problems as well as to their talents and to cope with everyday problems. Tonic also intends to begin a doctoral program later in 1976 out of which he hopes to produce a formal textbook for the study of criminal justice.

Mr. Tonic is also involved in politics. In the primary election of June 1976, he was elected to the post of Democratic County Committeeman of the North Ward, District 5, in Orange, New Jersey.

Superintendent of Schools
JOHNNY L. JONES
Miami, Florida

Dr. Johnny L. Jones's concern with providing "visible models of minority leadership for youngsters across the country" led him into the classroom then on to become Deputy Superintendent of the Dade County public school system in Florida.

Dr. Jones received his early education in Greenville, North Carolina, his place of birth. He attended Bethune-Cookman College, Daytona Beach, Florida, where he received a Bachelor of Arts degree in English in 1955.

Following a stint in the Air Force, Dr. Jones began to do his part to make education effective for youngsters. He became a teacher and counselor in Palmetto, a small town in Florida. During five years of teaching he ran an adult education program for the parents of his students. He felt adult education could bridge the gap in communication that existed between parents and their children. While he was teaching and running

Profiles in Black

this program he also pursued studies in guidance and school administration at several universities. His goal was achieved in 1964 when he received a Master's degree, and in 1966 when he received a doctorate in education from the University of Idaho.

In 1965, he was employed as an assistant principal at the predominantly Black Carver Junior High School in Dade County. Following that assignment, he became the assistant principal of another junior high school that had changed from an all-white to an all-Black student body. In these two assignments Dr. Jones felt that he "made some positive impact on those students who had envisioned life as nothing but a dead-end street." He relates that many of his former students have made their marks in life and have themselves become effective leaders.

When he became coordinator for research development and evaluation in the Dade County school system, Dr. Jones was responsible for providing program audits and evaluation on the federal programs that poured more than 27 million dollars into the Dade County school system. In this capacity he helped to design a model school in the inner city area. Called the Drew Middle School, it was hailed as the most innovative school in Florida. Its philosophy concentrates on the individual needs of its students. According to Dr. Jones, "both national and international visitors came to witness a facility which appeared to be twenty years ahead of its time."

As Director of Secondary Schools, Dr. Jones came in contact with schools that were undergoing desegregation. During this period, he recounts, suspension of students was on the increase and most of the students were Black. He was instrumental in imparting strong leadership qualities to the principals of the schools so that they were able to quell the number of suspensions.

Dr. Jones spent 1971 at Yale University Center for the Study of Education where he did a study to determine the impact that citizens have on school operations. After his studies at Yale, he became the first Black to be appointed Area Superintendent in the Dade County school system which comprised 42,000 students in 40 schools with over 100 principals and assistant principals.

At present, Dr. Jones is Deputy Superintendent of Schools, responsible for the administration of the nation's sixth largest school system.

Prior to Dr. Jones becoming Deputy Superintendent the rate of expulsions was high, particularly for minority students, which approximated some 150 per year and an excessive number of outdoor suspensions. Within the past two years, under his leadership, expulsions have decreased to only one, with at least a 60 per cent reduction in suspensions.

Now I await the rise of the Negro theater. Our folk music, having achieved world-wide fame, offers itself to the genius of the great individual American Negro composer who is to come. And within the next decade I expect to see the work of a growing school of colored artists who paint and model the beauty of dark faces and create with new technique the expression of their own soul-world. And the Negro dancers who will dance like flame and the singers who will continue to carry our songs to all who listen.... (1926)

—Langston Hughes

Poet, Playwright, Author

Automobile Dealer
PORTERFIELD WILSON
Detroit, Michigan

Porterfield Wilson was born in Nashville, Tennessee, and later moved to Detroit in 1956. As with most Blacks looking for work in Detroit, he began his career at the Old Dodge Main Auto Factory. Finding this job unfulfilling, he became a clerk in a drugstore at night. His exceptional selling ability was noted and one of his customers, Angelo Ricci, encouraged him to be an automobile salesman. In early 1962, he joined Commes and Ricci, a Plymouth dealer. He recalls that it was a period when Blacks could sell only to Blacks, when civil rights demonstrations were not widespread.

Chrysler enlisted Porterfield Wilson by encouraging him to take on a dealership that carried a full line of Chrysler products. In September 1962, he joined Bill Snethkamp in Highland Park, Michigan, and became one of the industry's leading salesmen who had the distinction of being Chrysler's top national salesman. He won every award, including trips to Europe and the Caribbean islands.

By the Seventies, the auto dealership industry started to look for Blacks who had the expertise to own and manage dealerships. Porterfield Wilson elected to take on a Pontiac franchise on December 15, 1970. His first year, although a trial, was successful. He won the Pontiac Master Dealer Award in his second year, 1972, as well as for the following year.

His dealership employs over 50 persons and consists of an integrated management staff. Wilson claims the key to good business despite the highs and lows has been the dealership's concept of service: "Going the last mile and then some to please the customer."

Porterfield Wilson Pontiac has been listed in Black Enterprise List of Top 100 Black Businesses since its inception; its gross sales is over six million dollars annually. Wilson was cited for his contribution to the economic and social welfare of the Detroit and Michigan communities. He received the Booker T. Washington Business Achievement Award for 1975 and was given many citations for his civic and community work. He is married and he and his wife have one son.

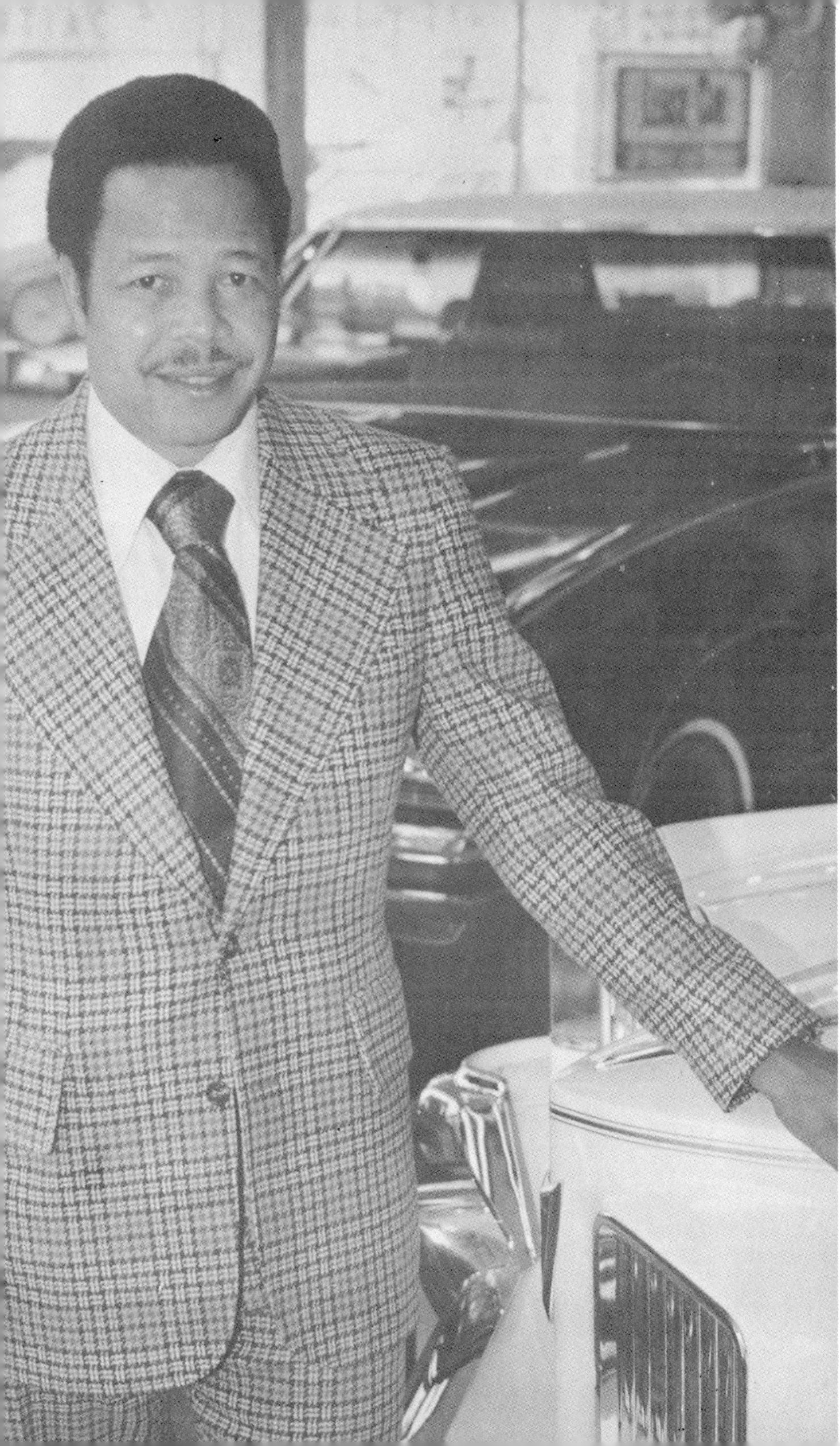

Businessman, Former Pro-football Player
WILLIE D. DAVIS
Los Angeles, California

Willie D. Davis knew a career in football was almost inevitable once he started piling up the points at Washington High School in Texarkana, Arkansas. He earned letters in three sports before graduating in 1952. Davis attended Grambling College in Louisiana, where he was captain of the football team. Davis made the Dean's lists from 1955-56, majoring in industrial arts. with minors in mathematics and physical education. He was president of the Kappa Alpha Psi fraternity and a member of the Lettermen's Club and the Interdormitory Council while at Grambling.

He spent twelve years with the National Football League, two years with the Cleveland Browns and ten years with the Green Bay Packers. He was selected to All-Pro teams for six years and took part in six divisional championships and five world championships as captain of the Packers's defensive unit. Off-season he taught school in Cleveland, Ohio.

Davis returned to school to do graduate work at Western Reserve University in Cleveland, Ohio, earning 15 hours of graduate credit in education.

He then began working for the Joseph Schlitz Brewing Company in sales and public relations, a job that really interested him and induced him to return to graduate school, this time the University of Chicago. He received his Master's in Business Administration in 1968, concentrating in marketing and personnel management as well as in industrial relations. Davis decided not to go back to teaching, but started his own business in February 1970. He is the owner and operator of the Willie Davis Distributing Company, utilizing his sales and public relations experiences and wisdom that he has gained with the Los Angeles County task force, LA Explorers (Boy Scouts), as director and board member of the West Adams Community Hospital. He is also a member of the South Shore Youth Committee.

He serves on the board of directors of the Joseph Schlitz Brewing Company, the first Black and second nonfamily member to be appointed.

Profiles in Black

Civic Leader
CATHERINE LEWIS MONTGOMERY
San Diego, California

Catherine Lewis Montgomery began her public service career while attending Howard University, Washington, D.C. After moving to San Diego, California, she was employed as an administrative assistant at the Navy Electronics Laboratory, a research and development branch of the U.S. Navy. She later became personnel director and administrative services director of the Economic Opportunity Commission of San Diego County. This position provided practical experience for her subsequent occupation as a Commissioner charged with the enforcement of the state's Fair Employment Practices and Fair Housing Acts during the last seven years.

She has been interested and involved for may years in civil rights and has served in various volunteer positions dealing with social, political and economic development of the minority community of San Diego. She is a member of the San Diego Urban League and the board of directors of the NAACP. As president of the San Diego Links, she has offered financial support to the Congress of Racial Equality. She has contributed to the San Diego Women for Better Education for Minority Students. She was the organizer of the mothers' auxiliary at the San Diego Girls Club and was president of the board of the San Diego Girls Club and is now on the National Board of the Girls Club of America, Inc. Catherine Montgomery has participated in non-partisan-voter education workshops, co-chaired and organized headquarters for various ballot propositions as well as coordinated fundraising events dealing with major civic, charitable and business organizations in the minority community. Ms. Montgomery enjoys working with people, and her concern for the problems of human beings has been demonstrated at the local, state and national levels.

The above activities led to appointments by the Board of Supervisors to Mental Health Services Advisory Board 1968-72; by the Mayor to the City Planning Commission (the first Black and the only woman at the time) 1966-73; and the President's Advisory Council on Minority Business Enterprises from 1972-75.

Her broad community experience and the training she received at the National Institute of Public Affairs to study problems of the cities earned her an Associateship in Urban Affairs in 1968 after which she became a consultant in urban affairs. She has participated on panels dealing with leadership training, community planning and development, urban affairs, career development for women and minorities. She has lectured on affirmative action in employment and housing and on laws regarding discrimination, before business associations, educational institutions, civil rights groups, women's organizations and city and county municipalities. She has also lectured to classes at the University of California on land-use controls and regional planning.

Profiles in Black

Along with the demands of her civil rights career and extensive volunteer positions, she maintained a home for her son, Alpha LeVon, Jr., who attended the University of California at both San Diego and Davis.

Corporate Director
ROBERT J. KEYES
Burbank, California

Robert Keyes was born on a farm in Bakersfield, California, the fourth of seven children. When he was 11 years old, his father became extremely ill and young Robert had to learn to work the fields and drive the trucks and tractors. Four years later his father died. His mother was so saddened that she practically gave away the farm and moved the family to the city.

While in high school Robert did all kinds of odd jobs, picking cotton, fruits, vegetables; pitching watermelons from sunrise to sunset; cutting grapes; shining shoes. His future looked very bleak until Paul Platz, his high school football coach, "kindled an interest in going to college." The other person to strongly influence him was Bob McCutcheon, football coach at Antelope Valley Junior College, who persuaded him to enroll in 1955. The first day of football practice offered a piece of memorable advice from Coach McCutcheon: "Every year everybody has to try out for my ball club all over again. No spots are picked out for anyone from the previous season." The talk bolstered the young man, giving him the courage to realize fresh opportunities and motivating him to achieve Junior College All American for two years. He played pro football with the San Francisco 49ers and the Oakland Raiders.

In 1956, he was the leading junior college scorer in the U.S. Keyes went on to the University of San Diego but quit to join the Marine Corps. A few months later two major illnesses in his immediate family forced him to quit the services to support them by making money in the more lucrative professional football field. But his mother insisted that he finish his college education—which he did in 1962.

Thereafter, Robert Keyes taught accounting and coached football and track at St. Augustine High School in San Diego and married in 1960. An intense need to broaden his interests found him involved in a mayoral campaign in which his candidate won. To further support his family, Keyes took on selling insurance part time. His selling was so successful that he left teaching in 1966 to go into insurance full time.

In 1967, Keyes was invited by Gov. Ronald Reagan to head the newly established Community Relations Program which involved being liaison in labor, housing, poverty programs and race relations as well as being the State Human Relations Officer.

In 1972, Robert Keyes became Corporate Director of Urban Affairs, a position he currently holds. He is working to promote minority and women's recruiting for salaried personnel throughout the country.

Profiles in Black

Bishop
VINTON RANDOLPH ANDERSON
Birmingham, Alabama

Bishop Vinton Randolph Anderson was born and raised by foster parents in Somerset, Bermuda, and received the call to the ministry in 1946, and a year later moved to the United States. He did his undergraduate work at Wilberforce University and obtained his Master of Divinity at Payne Theological Seminary—both schools in Ohio—and his Master of Arts degree at Kansas University, Lawrence. He is an alumnus of the Urban Training Center for Christian Mission, Chicago, Illinois.

He had a fruitful ministry in Topeka, Kansas, and in St. Louis, Missouri, for eight years. He took augmented studies at the Urban Training Center for Christian Mission in Chicago, and at the Yale Divinity School of Continuing Education. Bishop Anderson was elected in 1972 to the episcopacy of the African Methodist Episcopal Church, combining his commitment as a theologian with a total involvement in his community. At present Bishop Anderson is serving as Bishop of the Ninth Episcopal District of Alabama.

Among Bishop Anderson's civic and community contributions are: chairman of the board of directors of the Wichita Urban League; the first Black president of the Ministerial Associations of Parsons and Lawrence, Kansas; the first Black chairman of the trustee board of the Wichita Council of Churches. He has also participated in CORE's car-service program in St. Louis and served as chairman of St. Louis's Interdenominational Center for Urban Affairs, as secretary to the Missouri Council of Churches and as president of the Inter-Church Association.

In the economic affairs of his community, Bishop Anderson was a co-founder and co-developer of one of the first Black-owned and operated chain of supermarkets. He is chairman of the Vanguard Bond and Mortgage board of directors and a promotor of federally sponsored housing in his community. He has served as chairman of the board of directors for Primm Gardens Housing.

Bishop Anderson was a member of the four-person panel appointed by the World Council of Churches in 1972 to implement a program to combat racism, a fact-finding mission sent to New Zealand and Australia. Currently he is serving as Chairman of the Commission on the Worship for Consultation on Church Union. He has attended the World Methodist Council meetings three times as a delegate.

He holds a Doctor of Divinity degree from Paul Quinn College, Waco, Texas, and Doctor of Humanities from Wilberforce University.

Bishop Anderson and his wife, Vivienne, have four sons.

Profiles in Black

Professional Air Traffic Controller
KATY HARPER
Longview, Texas

Katy Harper came into air traffic control work by chance. She says, "A girl friend told me they were conducting tests for air traffic controllers and, although I wasn't sure what an air traffic controller was at the time I decided to find out." She passed her test and started her career, working part time at Townsfield Tower in Texas. Discovering a natural aptitude, combined with a willingness to learn about the world of aviation, she received three months' training in Tyler, Texas, her birthplace, and a year's probationary assignment at Gregg Airport, Longview. Ms. Harper praises the SF-150 program which gave her and others a chance at the profession. She has a smooth working relationship with her fellow controllers and except for a few minor problems in the past with pilots, she "has a very fulfilling career that she thoroughly loves and enjoys, although the responsibility of being a controller is a large one." She has the distinction of being the first Black and first female controller in East Texas.

Katy Harper is not a hard-core feminist, but her philosophy is, "Whatever you want to do, do it." She claims that her basic education was very sound, and that she worked as a secretary at the local chapter of the Human Relations Council through her first two years at Texas College in Tyler, and had scholarships and government loans to help her through. Upon graduation in 1970, she was given an aptitude test for recruitment of minorities and the Federal Aviation Administration selected her for part-time work and the training program. There was further training after that at the FAA Academy in Oklahoma City. At that time, newly divorced and supporting a son, she looked forward to a rewarding career that would also offer her a means of earning a good living.

"When I became a controller, I was somewhat a celebrity in my home town," she says. "But I have always felt that I have a special obligation. The better I do my job, the easier it will be for the next woman to make it."

Ms Harper was instrumental in the formation of the first local chapter of the Professional Air Traffic Controllers Organization in Longview and is its secretary. She also has found support and friendship not only from her fellow controllers but also from the PATCO local president Tom Hollis, who has been a strong friend. "It's nice to know there is someone in your corner. There is a security in a union that we all need."

Profiles in Black

Poet
EVERETT NATHANIEL CONLEY
Berlin, New Jersey

Everett Nathaniel Conley attributes his success as a poet to his grandmother, Mrs. Dorothy Conley Elam. His grandmother, who is a teacher, recognized very early in Conley's life that her grandson would someday use his gift with words to enlighten and entertain others.

Everett recalls that each Christmas he received a book from his grandmother that told of the achievements and struggles of other Black people. He cites these gifts and the thought behind them as the key motivating factor in the development of his talent as a writer.

In 1971, Everett's poem "I" was published on the front cover of the October issue of the *Negro History Bulletin,* an organ of the Association for the Study of Afro-American Life and History based in Washington, D.C. Publication of his poem had the same euphoric effect on Everett as it would on any young Black writer who has seen his work published for the first time. Since his initiation in publishing, Conley's career as an established poet has grown by leaps and bounds. His former sixth-grade teacher was so impressed by his work that he personally edited and prepared a collection of Conley's work for publication. That collection is now being used in many schools in New Jersey.

Another collection entitled *A Slice of Black Living* is distributed by Conlam Enterprise, a company owned by his grandmother. Ms. Cecilia Brown, a supervisor of education in the Camden, New Jersey, school system, says of *A Slice of Black Living,* "Thoughts that live and breathe and words that burn, this is the manner in which Thomas Grey, the English poet, described a good poem, and frankly speaking, this is an excellent description of Mr. Conley's first collection of poems. After reading *A Slice of Black Living,* one cannot help but feel that there is an illimitable store of imagination and moral truth in this collection from which lessons of worth can be learned."

The Camden, New Jersey, YMCA presented Conley with a trophy in 1973. A biographical directory entitled *Living Black American Authors,* published in 1973 by R. R. Bowker Company, recognized his works.

Profiles in Black

Janitorial Maintenance Operator
NATHANIEL D. WILLIAMS
Washington, D.C.

Nathaniel D. Williams, Chief Executive Officer and President of Clean-Rite Maintenance Company, Inc., in Washington, D.C., fulfills the old saying "It takes a lot of hard work to succeed." With part-time and full-time positions and accepting additional responsibilities, Nathaniel Williams was made manager while working with another firm and became involved with all aspects of the company. However, the realization that he was generating for someone else compelled him to venture out on his own into the maintenance business.

Nathaniel Williams started his own business in Washington, D.C., as a building janitorial maintenance contractor. As with most minority business men and women, insufficient working capital proved to be a problem. The money for equipment, supplies and fulfilling payroll commitments for employees was badly needed. The Black Economic Union (BEU, which is currently known as the Washington Black Economic Union Development Company) guaranteed 80 per cent of the $1,500 loan received by Mr. Williams in December 1969.

Clean-Rite has become an operation that is steadily growing. The company has over 300 employees who perform jobs at Goddard Space Flight Center, Andrews Air Force Base and Fort Belvoir; window washing in the buildings of the Departments of State, Commerce, and Justice and the General Services Administration.

In 1972, Clean-Rite was selected by the GSA to provide all janitorial maintenance services required by the Inaugural Committee, for all federal facilities. In 1970, *Black Enterprise* Magazine named Clean-Rite as one of the top 100 Black firms that grossed in excess of a million dollars.

In 1975, Mr. Williams created the National Combined Services Association. NCSA is a trade association of janitorial maintenance companies, organized through his efforts to better the conditions for minorities operating in the industry. Their primary purpose is to upgrade the janitorial maintenance industry and aid its members in competing effectively in the market.

Early in 1975, he also formed another company, E-ZEE Chemical & Supplies. E-ZEE is actively engaged in the wholesale-distribution and retailing of industrial chemical supplies and equipment. Again Mr. Williams has successfully created another viable minority enterprise. Projections for future growth and expansion are part of the immediate plans for these much-needed businesses.

Nathaniel Williams was born in Fort Mott, South Carolina, and in his teens moved to Washington, D.C., where he continued his education. He attended Temple University, Philadelphia, Pennsylvania, Champlain College, Plattsburgh, New York; and Ithaca College, New York, where

Profiles in Black

he majored in physical education. However, he was strongly interested in business administration and took courses at Howard and American universities, both in D.C., concentrating on janitorial maintenance. He also gained a diploma in drafting from Letcher's Art Center and is currently enrolled at the University Without Walls in Amherst, Massachusetts.

Besides lecturing to business college students, he is active with the Police Boys Club, the YMCA and in work with disadvantaged youth. He was also a recent participant in the photographic exhibition of outstanding Black Americans, sponsored by the Detroit Bicentennial Commission.

Very soon after I went to live with Mr. and Mrs. Auld, she very kindly commenced to teach me the A*B*C. After I learned this, she assisted me in learning to spell words of three or four letters. Just at this point of my progress, Mr. Auld found out what was going on, and at once forbade Mrs. Auld to instruct me further, telling her, among other things, that it was unlawful, as well as unsafe, to teach a slave to read. (1845)
—Frederick Douglass
Orator, Abolitionist, Editor

Cardiologist
EDITH C. REID
New York, New York

Although Edith C. Reid was born in Atlantic City, New Jersey, she considers herself a New Yorker because when she was three months old her mother Anne was widowed, and moved to New York City. Her mother proved to be the guiding light in Edith Reid's life, "a source of deep love, inspiration and firm discipline" and a woman who expected her daughter to be a high achiever. As a result of her mother's encouragement, young Edith pursued musical training.

Dr. Reid says she understands how young people can have difficulties making career decisions because she, too, went through the same changes. She started out as a history major with a biology minor at Hunter College and changed to a biology major with a chemistry minor in her sophomore year. In her third year, she realized that she wanted to study medicine. She considered pathology because she found the final information obtained from an autopsy to be fascinating. However, she says that "one of my life's enthusiasms has been my true interest in and affection for people. I knew that I had to be involved with people."

She entered Meharry Medical College which was her first all-Black school experience. After graduation from Meharry she returned to New York City to become the first Black intern at Brookdale Hospital in Brooklyn. Since then Dr. Reid has worked at Flower and Fifth Avenue Hospital, the Chest Clinic of the New York City Department of Health, Jamaica Hospital and the Carter Community Health Center, as well as maintaining her own practice in cardiology.

She is a member of the Queens Clinical Society and has played a vital role in aiding the organization in seeking solutions to community problems. She is also a member of the National Medical Association, the Empire State Medical Society and the American Medical Association. She is an Associate Fellow of the American College of Chest Physicians.

Dr. Reid was instrumental in the fund proposal for the hypertension control program in Southeast Queens, New York, the first time that a free standing health facility was funded by the Department of Health, Education and Welfare.

In 1974, she became the first female to be appointed by the Board of Regents of the State University of New York for the State Board of Medicine, and she remains the only Black member. She also has been appointed project director for the detection and treatment of hypertensive diseases at the Carter Community Health Center, the program which she steered to final funding.

She was involved with community efforts to raise defense funds for two students jailed in Florida during the early days of the sit-ins and when the students were released, Dr. Reid recalls, CORE sponsored their trip to New York.

Dr. Reid is married to an attorney, John Lee Edmonds.

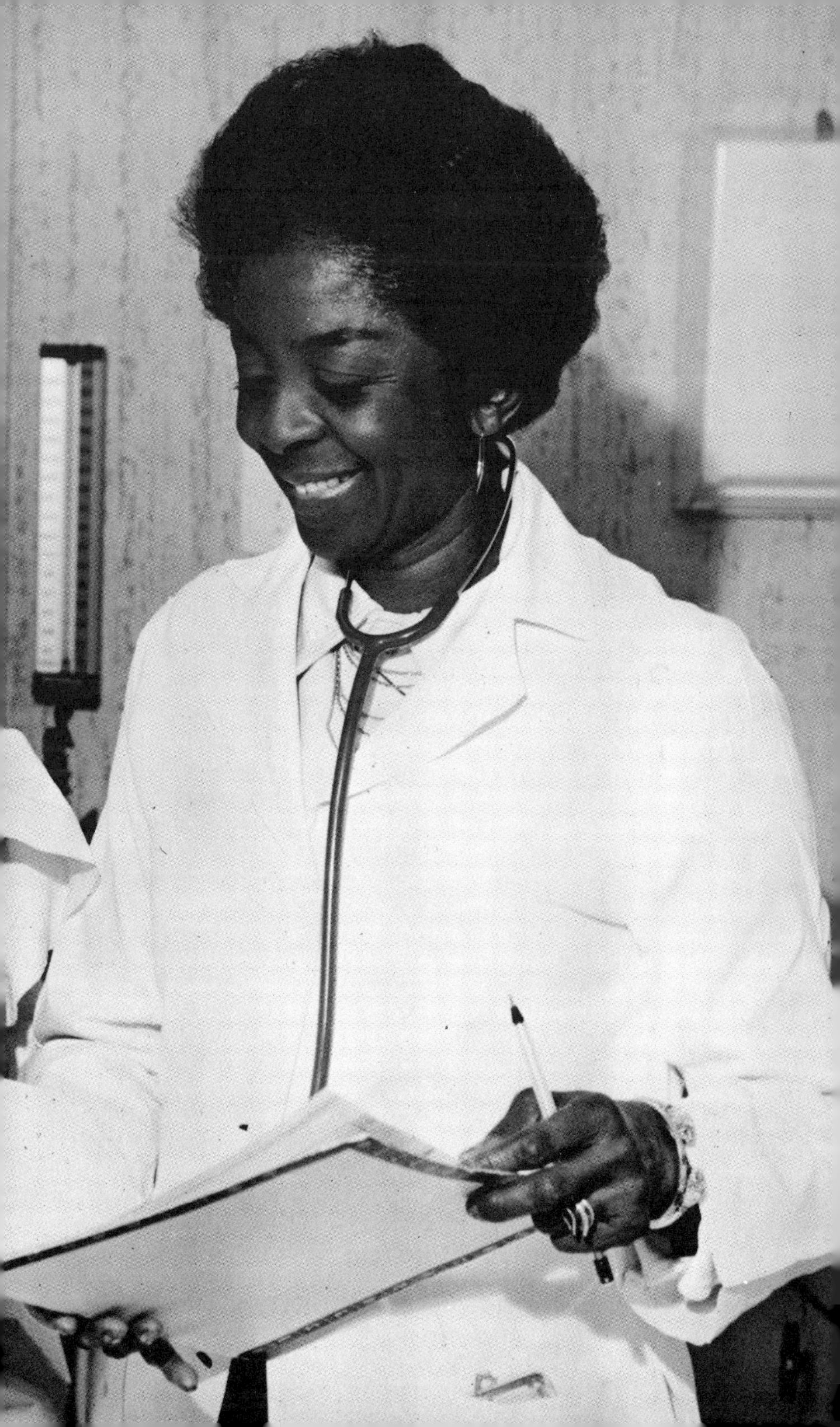

Contractor
JOE W. KIRVEN
Dallas, Texas

Profiles in Black

Joe W. Kirven is the founder and president of the ABCO Building Maintenance Company, Inc., based in Dallas, Texas. It is the second largest Black-owned and employed business in the State of Texas, and until 1972 was the largest minority-owned business and employer in Texas.

In 1968, Mr. Kirven was chosen by the Texas Junior Chamber of Commerce as one of five outstanding young men in Texas—the first and only minority member ever chosen. For six years running he was chosen by various local business and professional organizations as the Businessman of the Year. He has been recognized by *Ebony* magazine in 1969 and 1971 as one of the Outstanding Businessmen in the Southwest.

Joe Kirven was one of the original members of the President's Advisory Committee on Minority Business Enterprises and was also the Chairman of the Task Force on Technical and Managerial Assistance.

Along with Sam Wyly Ventures Advisers, Inc., Joe Kirven founded a nonprofit corporation to help minority businesses both technically and financially. In 1970, Ventures Advisers, Inc., as the counselling organization was called, received funding from the Office of Minority Business Enterprises. Mr. Kirven was the corporation's first president.

Besides his interest and assistance in helping minority businesses, Joe Kirven has served three terms as president of the Dallas Negro Chamber of Commerce as well as serving as area captain for Circle Ten of the Boy Scouts of America. In 1970, he was the second Black to serve on the Dallas school board.

Joe Kirven is married and he and his wife have one teen-aged daughter.

Artist, Teacher, Lecturer
FAITH RINGGOLD
New York, New York

After receiving a Bachelor of Arts and a Master of Fine Arts from the City College of New York, Faith Ringgold taught art from elementary to high school levels in New York City. She describes the 17 years spent on teaching as some of her best learning years. She was involved with a program called More Effective Schools (MES) that ended—having become "an effective and a beneficial tool for Black students."

While she was teaching she continued to paint. In the early years watercolors was her medium. In the early Sixties she found a distinctive style to call her own. In 1961, she traveled through Europe to study the masterpieces that she had read about; however, she saw exhibits of African art that was to have a marked influence on the development of her style.

Ms. Ringgold describes her first style of painting as super realism, developed in 1963, relating the socio-political direction of Black people during the Sixties. In 1967, she began to paint the large murals that were exhibited at her first one-woman show at the Spectrum Gallery in New York City. One of her murals is permanently installed at the Women's House of Detention at Rikers Island.

Faith Ringgold's desire to express herself through art was not an easy road to travel; as a matter of fact, it caused her to be arrested. She and 200 other artists participated in an exhibit of works based on the American flag at the Judson Church in 1970. At this point she was not content with merely making statements in her work because she felt she was not reaching Black people. She decided to create posters of subject matter that was more relevant, one of which is the acclaimed "United States of Attica." She also creates masks on the African art form originated by African women, and has also done a series of paintings dedicated to the Black Woman and sculpture of human figures made of foam rubber and coconut heads. Most of her paintings are framed in cloth, a style she refers to as "Tibetan Tanks," that makes her collection portable besides being less expensive. She is currently teaching African crafts at the Bank Street College and at the Museum of Natural History.

Besides her art, Faith Ringgold has dedicated her life to the articulation of Black womanhood. Being Black, female and an artist has created the most difficult obstacles she has had to overcome. She uses art as her weapon against racial and sexual discrimination.

Profiles in Black

Businessman
AL HOLLINGSWORTH
Los Angeles, California

In the process of selecting their life goals, many people are inspired by a number of things—self-incentive, their families' encouragement or education. But Al Hollingsworth's inspiration came from a "blow" to the head. During Al Hollingsworth's two-season career with the New York Giants he had a football accident that caused him to change course by using his business acumen in building his two million-dollar corporations.

A young, dynamic personality, Al is the son of Ruth and A.D. Hollingsworth, formerly of Jackson, Mississippi, who migrated in 1947 to Omaha, Nebraska, where Al attended grade school and high school. He then attended the University of Colorado in Boulder and obtained his undergraduate and his Master's degree in psychology in 1964. He later earned his Master's in Business Administration from the University of Seattle, Washington. Hollingsworth was employed by the Zellerbach Paper Company for two years and for an additional two years with Fiberboard, where he acquired an abundance of expertise in the sales area. Because he worked his way through school, he believes that the simultaneous experiences of work and education offered him a wider perspective on his life and his future.

Al Hollingsworth thinks he made some very wise investments in IBM and Xerox Corporation stocks. With his acute business awareness he started his own million-dollar corrugated box manufacturing company. Using his aptitude, he created a demand for raw materials such as corrugated board, developed the concept for Sheet Plant Corporation in 1970 and formed a second million-dollar corporation, SQWAT, which deals in cardboard and plastic furniture along with pictorial modules. He plans to open a chain of boutiques and beauty-care centers, the latter to be operated with ultramodern, technological methods of beauty treatment. These shops will be situated in Los Angeles, Washington, D.C., and other areas and they will be run in conjunction with a major department store corporation.

Besides, being a dynamic businessman, the multifaceted Al Hollingsworth is also involved in community affairs. He is one of the three founders and a board member of the Black Business Men's Associates and was the president from 1974-75. Each week this association brings to the community seminars to educate business men and women on economics and business growth.

In 1972, Al Hollingsworth created the "Hot Seat," a BBMA program, made up of top business executives from major companies throughout the country. "Hot Seat" focuses on the affirmative action programs and is aired on various spot announcements throughout Los Angeles.

Profiles in Black

He was also instrumental in forming "Salute to Student Lunches," a program geared to educating youths on their roles in this society, encouraging them to absorb as much education as possible, and to apply it to their individual goals and ambitions in order to obtain successful and gratifying careers. He claims that not all the superstars like Sammy Davis, Jr., or Jim Brown are necessarily the success models as Black leaders, but that the "bottom-line people or people who sign the check line" can be equally effective as examples of successful Blacks.

Statistician
WM. LARRY LUCAS
Suitland, Maryland

This unusual career of being a minority statistics programs specialist stemmed, according to Wm. Larry Lucas, "from having a mother and father who believed so strongly in education and from living in a community that encouraged and supported me as an individual. That gave me an extra incentive to try and advance to the best of my ability."

Born in Mississippi in the community of Hopewell, in Collins, Larry Lucas attended elementary, junior high and high school in Collins and went on to receive his Bachelor of Science degree in education from Jackson State College, Mississippi. He also attended the School of Radio and Television at the University of Detroit, Michigan.

Mr. Lucas's career was multifaceted and varied before he arrived at his present-day occupation. He was a personnel specialist in the U.S. Air Force; he was a disc jockey with radio station WOKJ in Jackson, Mississippi; he did news reporting and disc jockeying with WCHD-FM station in Detroit; and he was a statistics consultant with Seymour and Lundy public relations firm, also in Detroit. In 1966, he joined the Bureau of the Census of the Department of Commerce as a data collection specialist. The aims of the Minority Statistics Program with which Mr. Lucas is now involved are to equalize coverage of minority populations with other segments of the population in the U.S., to inform members of minority populations of the availability and significance of statistics and to obtain the recommendations from these minority populations for improving coverage and quality of data for the 1980 census.

In addition to his regular census duties, Mr. Lucas was appointed as an equal opportunity counselor. He has served two years on the board of governors of Shaw College in Detroit. He is a member of the Public Relations Society of America.

Mr. Lucas is single and spends his time traveling extensively.

Profiles in Black

County Commissioner, Minister
EDWARD T. GRAHAM
Miami, Florida

Profiles in Black

Reverend Edward T. Graham was not really interested in participating in politics until the Miami City Commission had difficulty filling the vacant position of county commissioner. When Reverend Graham's name came up as a possible candidate on the Metropolitan Dade County Commission, he was appointed. In the fall of 1971, he ran for a full term and received the highest number of votes.

Reverend Graham received his elementary and secondary education in South Carolina. He obtained his Bachelor of Science degree from Benedict College, South Carolina, in 1928 and his Master's degree in sociology from Columbia University, New York City, in 1929. He attended New York City's Union Theological Seminary and received his Doctor of Divinity degree from St. Andrew's Seminary, London, England, in 1962.

His work career began in 1930 when he worked in a manufacturing firm in New York City for three years, then to administrative work with the Department of Social Services from 1933-39. The year 1939 was a magic number because of the World's Fair in New York. Reverend Graham did public relations work for the Fair. From there he branched out into other areas of civil and social work such as being program director for the Brooklyn YMCA from 1939-41 and executive director of the United States Service Organization (USO) in Camp Croft, South Carolina, and in Miami from 1943-45. In Miami he was the founder and executive director of the Greater Miami Urban League. He became the minister for the Mount Zion Baptist Church in 1948 and currently holds the same position.

Reverend Graham is involved in numerous organizations such as the Southern Christian Leadership Conference of which he is a current board member, the Florida Council on Human Relations of which he is treasurer, the Miami Chapter of the American Civil Liberties Union, the Dade County Criminal Justice Advisory Council of which he is a board member at the request of Gov. Reubin O'D. Askew.

Among the many citations Reverend Graham has received are the Omicron Delta Kappa key from the University of Miami and the Silver Beaver Award from the Boy Scouts of America—both in 1975. From the Greater Miami Urban League he was given the Whitney M. Young Memorial Humanitarian Award in 1971, as well as dozens of other medals and awards of distinction.

Chemist
BERNARDO TAYLOR
Flushing, New York

Bernardo Taylor was born in St. Thomas, the U.S. Virgin Islands. He was one of twelve children, three of whom lived with their father, Clarence. Clarence Taylor, the official photographer of the Island, had a long-term effect on the careers of Bernardo and his brother Alvin. Young Bernardo attended school until he was 15 working from age 10 at the A.H. Riise Apothecary, concurrently helping his father.

Bernardo Taylor came to New York on August 1927. Two years later, he found jobs as a biochemical technician at New York University College of Dentistry, with the aid of brother Alvin who was already there, and as a clinical technologist at Columbus Hospital. While taking night courses at the City College of New York, he began work with the Department of Biochemistry and the Department of Bacteriology. With the last department he did chemical research, developing methods of clinical analysis in the detection of certain mineral elements in body sera (fluids). One of few Blacks working there, he found the job low paying. During his lengthy career at NYU, Mr. Taylor got married. After his wife gave birth to two children, she joined him in the same department, taking over his job when he retired from his post.

In 1958, he joined Fotochrome, a Kodak-licensed photofinishing company, as the chief chemical analyst, remaining with the firm for over ten years. In his new capacity, he analyzed different photographic development solutions for their performance and development capability. He also worked as a photographic processor at ATCO Scientific Laboratories, a company that specialized in scientific (medical) photography, of which his brother Alvin was president.

Later he went to work for Royaltone in New York City, another photofinishing company, for four and a half years, and set up its laboratory, no mean accomplishment. After Royaltone, he worked briefly at Hament Corporation. Currently, he is the director of chemical control of the Chrome Division of Strome Connecticut Corporation, now relocated in New Jersey.

Mr. Taylor holds a certificate to practice clinical chemistry and hematology in New York City hospitals. He is a member of the American Chemical Society, the American Association for the Advancement of Science and the Society of Motion Pictures and Television Engineers.

Profiles in Black

Real Estate Developer
NATHANIEL S. RUSSELL
Tucson, Arizona

Nathaniel S. Russell was born in Long Branch, New Jersey. He received his primary and secondary school education in Jersey and went on to Monmouth College from 1955-61, obtaining an Associate Arts degree, then going on to the University of Arizona in Tucson, where he majored in business law. He continued his studies at the National Housing Specialist Institute in Washington, D.C., and graduated in 1971.

He received his real estate broker's license in June 1958, his insurance agent's license in 1963 and his contractor's license for heavy construction and general engineering in 1968.

Nathaniel Russell's accomplishments refute the old saying "Jack of all trades, master of none." Although he worked in various fields and occupations until 1968, there was a method to his "madness." He ventured into the development of low-income housing on a large scale, an area that was denied to minority contractors until the 1968 Fair Housing Act. From that year on he worked hard until he shaped a well-organized development company.

Currently a developer-builder with Builders Urban Development Company, Russell hopes to provide better housing, to train and employ minority and low-income workers so they can be financially successful through working at the things "they like best" and to seek self-satisfaction through the achievement of immediate goals.

The 1974 Community Bill has enabled Russell to initiate new programs, and he has great expectations for national growth. Put in his own words, "I sincerely hope that more Blacks will be oriented to the vocation of real estate development. The possibilities and potentials are both exciting and compensating."

Nathaniel Russell serves on the board of many state and national organizations. He is on the board of directors of the Southern Arizona Home Builders Association and the National Association of Minority Contractors; he is executive director of the Southwest Area Minority Contractors and is a member of the National Association of Real Estate Brokers and the United Mortgage Bankers Association. His involvement in community and professional areas is extensive.

He and his wife Frances have seven children: Roxanne (who is married), Richard, Michael, Sharon, David, Garry and Nathaniel, Jr.

Profiles in Black

He told me, "Malcolm, you ought to be thinking about a career. Have you been giving it thought?"
The truth is, I hadn't. I never have figured out why I told him, "Well, yes, sir, I've been thinking I'd like to be a lawyer." Lansing certainly had no Negro lawyers—or doctors either—in those days, to hold up an image I might have aspired to. All I really knew for certain was that a lawyer didn't wash dishes, as I was doing.
Mr. Ostrowski looked surprised.... "Malcolm, one of life's first needs is for us to be realistic. Don't misunderstand me, now. We all here like you, you know that. But you've got to be realistic about being a nigger. A lawyer—that's no realistic goal for a nigger. You need to think about something you <u>can</u> be. You're good with your hands.... Everybody admires your carpentry shop work. Why don't you plan on carpentry?"

—Malcolm X

Black Nationalist Leader

Librarian
ESSIE CYNTHIA JENKINS
Jamaica, New York

Known to New Yorkers as "Cynthia" although her first name is Essie, Cynthia Jenkins was inspired by her sister who was a librarian for many years. Cynthia Jenkins herself has been a librarian for over 15 years. During her librarianship she founded many community groups because she encountered discrimination in library services "that exist directly or indirectly throughout the United States." Since she wanted to bring these discriminatory practices to the attention of the public, she helped to found the Black Librarians Caucus.

Mrs. Jenkins obtained her Bachelor of Arts in history from the University of Louisville, Kentucky, her Master of Arts in library science from Pratt Institute, Brooklyn, New York, and the Public Librarians Certificate from the State University of New York in 1966.

She began her career at the Brooklyn Public Library as Children's Books Librarian and since 1962 has been on staff with the Queens Borough Public Library. Recently, however, she has been concentrating on duties as branch manager of several units of the Queens Borough system.

Mrs. Jenkins is one of the founders of the Black Librarians Caucus and has been its chairman for five years. She organized the Social Concerns Committee of Springfield Gardens, an education action group, and was the chairman for over six years. She founded and was the first chairman of the Social Concerns Vendor Agency, an employment agency. She was a co-founder and has been a board member of the Springfield Gardens Community Service Agency. She is currently serving her second term as the Democratic State Committeewoman of the 29th Assembly District.

Cynthia Jenkins is married to an insurance broker who is the owner of the J.D. Jenkins Agency. They have one son who is studying for the United Methodist ministry at Boston University.

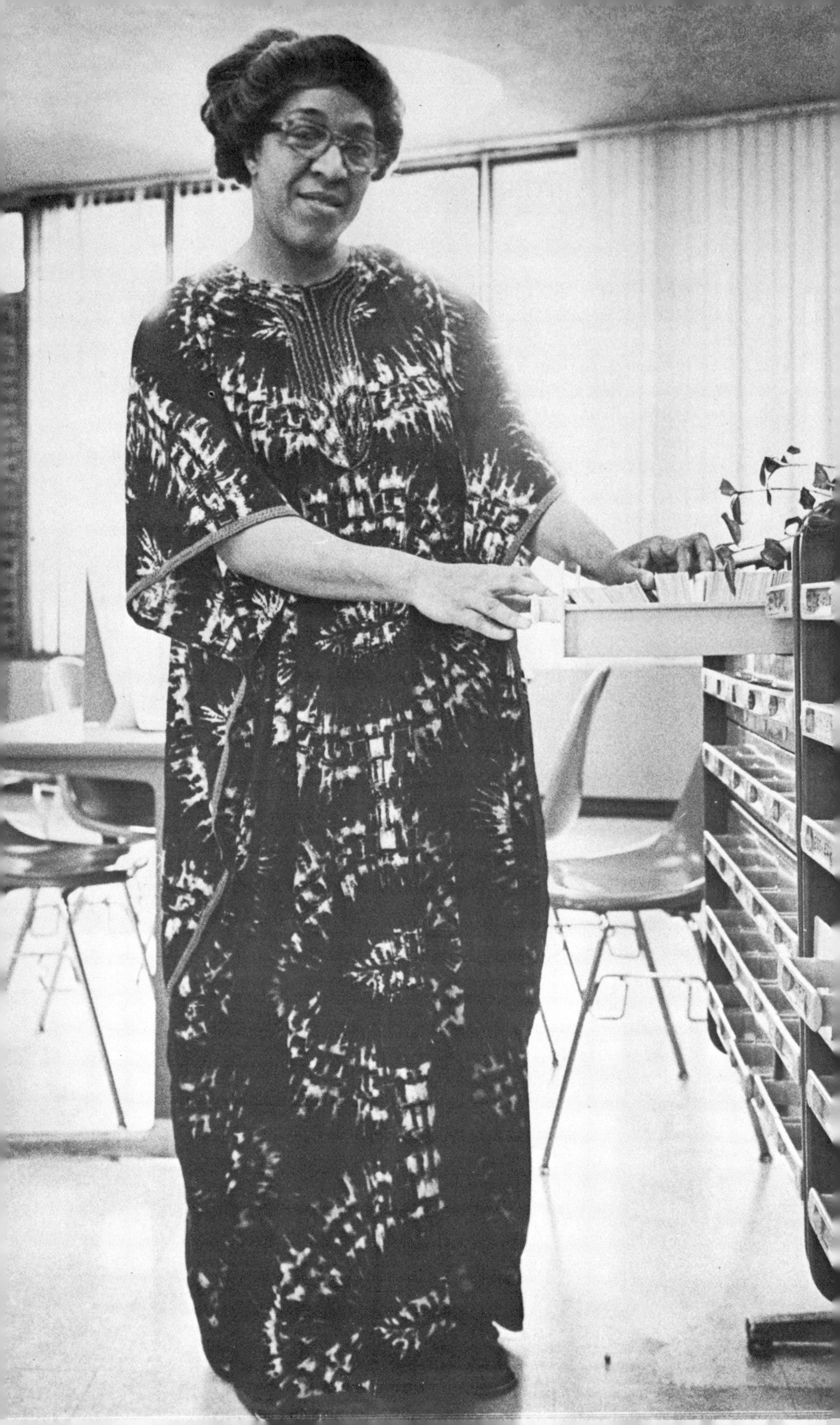

Newspaper Editor
CHARLES W. PORTER
Mobile, Alabama

Charles W. Porter began his career in 1962 as an instructor of journalism, English and speech at the Mobile County Training School where he was also director of publicity, staff photographer, assistant librarian, director of state-owned textbooks for the school. He says about this particular teaching experience, "With no journalistic experience but a lot of interest in journalism, I jumped at the opportunity to teach high school journalism after three years of teaching regular subjects. I worked hard and stayed ahead of my students. Together we built a popular class, a beautiful learning environment and a profitable high school newspaper."

From 1964-69, he was a part-time reporter for the weekly paper *Mobile Beacon* and from 1968, he was a newspaper reporter for the *Mobile Press-Register,* covering general news assignments. He worked in public relations at Tougaloo College, Mississippi, from 1970-71. He was publications editor with Northwestern University, Evanston, Illinois, a post he held from 1971-74. Currently, he is executive editor of the *Mobile Beacon,* a job that entails working with the circulation, advertising and even printing of the paper.

Charles Porter was born in Mobile, Alabama, and was educated in the Mobile public schools. He graduated from the Mobile County Training school in 1958. He did his undergraduate work at Bishop State Junior College, Mobile, and received his Bachelor of Science degree from Alabama State University, Montgomery, in 1962. He obtained his Master's degree in journalism at the University of Alabama in 1970. Mr Porter is a member of the American College Public Relations Association, the Education Writers Association and the National Council of College Publications Advisors, among others. He also participates with the Concerned Citizens for Police Reform (Chicago), Operation PUSH (People United to Save Humanity) and the Southern Christian Leadership Conference (SCLC). Mr. Porter is also a member of Sigma Delta Chi (journalism society), the Mobile Press Club, the Mobile Area Organization of Black Journalists—of which he is president—the Mobile Area Chamber of Commerce and the Alabama Press Association, among others.

Profiles in Black

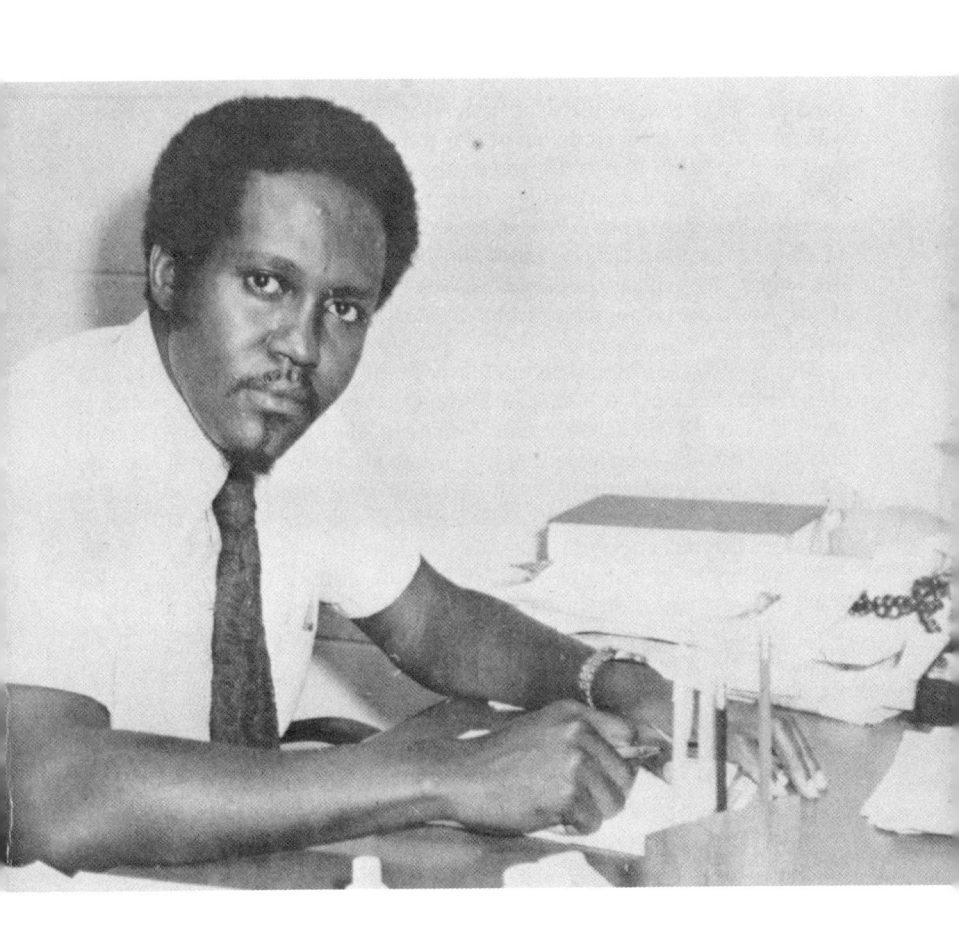

Newspaper Publisher
JOHN H. SENGSTACKE
Chicago, Illinois

John H. Sengstacke is the nephew of the late Robert Sengstacke Abbott who in 1905 was the founder of the Robert S. Abbott Publishing Company and of the *Chicago Defender*—the leading American Negro weekly newspaper of the day. Starting out in 1934 as vice president and general manager, Sengstacke became president of the publishing company in 1940. In 1956, John Sengstacke founded the *Chicago Daily Defender*—which has the largest daily Black paper circulation in the world—as well as the National Newspaper Publishers Association, of which he has served as president four times.

Mr. Sengstacke, in his sixties, is head of Sengstacke Newspapers, a group that includes the Michigan Chronicle Publishing Company, Detroit; the Tri-State Defender, Memphis, Tennessee; the Florida Courier, Miami; and the New Pittsburgh Courier Publishing Company. He is also the president of the Amalgamated Publishers, Inc., and director of the NNPA.

The recipient of numerous awards, Mr. Sengstacke was the first to receive the American Jewish Committee's Mass Media Award. He has also been accorded an honorary Doctor of Law degree from Elmhurst College, Illinois, and a Bachelor of Letters degree from Bethune-Cookman College, Daytona Beach, Florida, and Allen University, Columbia, South Carolina. He was awarded the Commander Star of Africa, bestowed by President Tubman of Liberia in 1958.

Mr. Sengstacke has been involved with a number of Presidential commissions, including the Assay Commission, the Board of Governors, the National Alliance of Businessmen's executive board and the New Advisory Committee on Equal Opportunity in the Armed Forces in 1962.

John Sengstacke attended grade school in Savannah, Georgia, and Knox Institute, Athens, Georgia. He graduated from Brick Junior College in 1929 and obtained his Bachelor of Science degree, majoring in business administration from Hampton Institute, Virginia, in 1934. After moving to Chicago, he took courses at Merganthaler Linotype School, the Chicago School of Printing, Northwestern University and Ohio State University.

Mr. Sengstacke is divorced and has three sons.

Profiles in Black

Civil Rights Specialist
LOUIS O. BRYSON
Atlanta, Georgia

Louis O. Bryson was born in 1936 in Chattanooga, Tennessee, and graduated from Tennessee State University with a Bachelor of Science degree (1960) and a Master of Science degree (1962). Because no Black had ever served in the capacity of psychological examiner in the Southeast, Bryson found that there was a dire need for a Black to fill that position in the public school system in Chattanooga. From 1961-66, he was the psychological examiner, the first Black to be on the central administrative staff of the city school system. In that position, he administered psychological tests to students to determine their intellectual potentials and their academic development. He also did remedial counseling with drop-out students to help them with their academic, social and economic problems.

In 1967, Louis Bryson moved to Atlanta, Georgia, where he worked with the Neighborhood Youth Corps (NYC) as a program development specialist—planning, initiating and coordinating programs that improved the chances for employment of the enrollees of the program. In October of the same year, he recalls, "I applied for a federal government job as the thrust for public school desegregation gained momentum and the federal government hired additional staff and set up a regional office. I was one of the first to be hired in the Atlanta Regional Office for Civil Rights of the Department of Health, Education and Welfare." He was later promoted to chief of the newly organized Higher Education Branch, an office that was created to enforce all civil rights laws pertaining to discrimination in institutions of higher education in the eighth state region. As a civil rights specialist, Louis Bryson reviews complaints of alleged discrimination practices in federal programs, researching for precedent—or past—cases to support and evaluate the current complaints. His job, so like the duties of an attorney, involves reviewing compliance reports, plans, court orders and other evidence, and meeting with representatives of other state regions to exchange information on requirements regarding legislation and regulation as stipulated by the government.

Mr. Bryson is a member of the National Association of Human Rights Workers and various civil rights organizations. He is married, and he and his wife have two children. He is a member of Warren United Methodist Church, where he serves on the administrative board and he sings with the John R. Gibson choir.

Profiles in Black

Employment Agent
WILLIAM H. SATTERFIELD
New York, New York

According to William H. Satterfield, "The turning point in my career was when my friend Mr. Bailey of the New York Transit Authority introduced me to community work in 1964, developing social programs for the Youth in Harlem under the Department of Parks and the New York City Youth Board." With the support of Claude Brown, the author, and Mrs. Cora Walker, the attorney, a group was formed to deal with housing and other issues in Harlem, including the Harlem Co-op Supermarket.

In 1967, Mr. Satterfield and Arthur Dunmeyer formed the People's Program under the aegis of the Urban League that dealt with drug rehabilitation upon which many other offshoot organizations were patterned in Atlanta, Detroit, Newark, San Francisco, Chicago and Washington, D.C. Mr. Satterfield's position was to teach services and to develop economic growth. He also aided in setting up the drug programs for Interfaith and Harlem hospitals in 1968. During the fall of that year he formed another youth program in the West Bronx called Morrisania Youth and Community Service Center, and in five years this program was considered the best street-based group and was heavily subsidized by the city. Because of his success, Mr. Satterfield was appointed by Mayor John Lindsay to the Board of Correction in which Satterfield along with attorney Haywood Burns and newscaster Geraldo Rivera managed to get Angela Davis released from solitary confinement from the Women's House of Dentention.

Since then William Satterfield has affiliated with the Board of Education, the Youth Detention Centers and the Urban Task Force (a special project for the Mayor). In 1971, Mr. Satterfield opened the first Black lobby office in Washington, D.C., to support street workers. He is also a planning consultant with the New York City Planning Commission.

In 1972, William Satterfield formed Satterfield Enterprises, Ltd., which is comprised of Singer Store dealerships and two employment agencies, the latter operation placing over 1,220 in 1975 or one out of every three clients—without charging any fee. Mr. Satterfield's agency maintains a contract with the Department of Labor and the New York City Department of Employment.

William Satterfield has been married 12 years to a wife who not only helped him to raise his children from a former marriage but also four of his parents' children and who "gave me the love and freedom to search and to operate the business."

Profiles in Black

Music Communicator
(BILL) WILL A. CHAPPELL
Hollywood, California

Bill Chappell is proud of the fact he was born and raised in Watts. He recalls lean days and hard times that made him stronger and more determined. Excelling in sports, he was offered several scholarships, and accepted one to the University of San Diego, where he majored in English.

Realizing the need for Black input in communications and media he worked at Columbia Broadcasting System for five years. Later he joined United Artists Records of America as director of artist relations. After five years inside the recording division of TransAmerica, he attained the prestigious position of assistant to the president. However, he was eager to be his own boss, to control his own life and destiny.

In 1973, he and Richard Roundtree formed Chaptree Production Company to produce some independent Black film and recordings. The following year found him on the board of directors of the Soul & Blues Academy which was the first Black-owned and controlled soul and blues award program to be videotaped for national viewing. Bill and partner Chuck Mann realized the need for a show of this type to support and honor Black talent. Chappell was eager to begin a new project that could serve the community. At the same time that he was struggling to keep the Soul & Blues Awards Academy alive, he was vice president of Cinema West Productions, a company that tried to get more Black input in Black programming on television.

The same year that he formed Chaptree, he established a Black trade music paper that began as an insert in *Phonograph Record Rock Magazine*. The idea was a conflict of interest with United Artists, so Chappell decided to devote all his time and energy to forming his own magazine, the first of its kind. Today *The Soul and Jazz Record Magazine* is a glossy-covered successful publication. Chappell has made the magazine an informative and a growing publication with the support of a small and dedicated staff of people who believe in what he is trying to build.

Profiles in Black

Source List

Contacts for Information

American Fund for Dental Education
211 East Chicago Avenue
Chicago, Ill. 60611

ASPO-Ford Foundation Minority Fellowships in Planning
American Society of Planning Officials
1313 East 60 Street
Chicago, Ill. 60632

College Admissions Assistance Center
Council of Higher Educational Institutions
461 Park Avenue South
New York, N.Y. 10016

Council on Legal Education Opportunity (CLEO)
2000 P Street, NW
Suite 300
Washington, D.C. 20036

The Earl Warren Legal Training Program
10 Columbus Circle
Suite 2030
New York, N.Y. 10019

Foundation Center
100 Connecticut Avenue, NW
Washington, D.C. 20036

    Contact the center for their 30 branches to apply for foundation grants.

Graduate Fellowships for Black Americans
National Fellowships Fund
795 Peachtree Street, NE
Suite 484
Atlanta, Ga. 30308

Martin Luther King, Jr., Fellowships
Woodrow Wilson National Fellowship Foundation
32 Nassau Street
Princeton, N.J. 08540

Counsel on law, medicine, social work, education, business administration, social sciences.

National Medical Fellowships, Inc. (for minority students)
250 West 57 Street
New York, N.Y. 10019

Public Service Materials Center
355 Lexington Avenue
New York, N.Y. 10016

List of fundraising sources.

U.S. Attorney General's office
Washington, D.C.

Write for published list of philanthropic organizations.

Books

Aid-to-Education Programs of Some Leading Business Concerns. Council for Financial Aid to Education, 6 East 45 Street, New York, N.Y. 10017.

Barron's Handbook of American Colleges. Woodbury, N.Y.: Barron's Educational Series, 1974.

Barron's Handbook of Junior and Community Colleges. Woodbury, N.Y.: Barron's Educational Series, 1974.

Cash for College. S. Robert Freeda. Englewood Cliffs, N.J.: Prentice-Hall, 1975.

Part I discusses financial aspects, evaluation of costs and loans, federal grant programs, scholarships and how to choose a school. Part II covers geographical fact finding on 2,994 educational institutions.

College Scholarships. David R. Turner. New York: Arco Books, 1968.
Part I covers plans, programs and possibilities. Parts II-V give tips on scholarship

233

Directory of Special Programs for Minority Group Members, 1974: Career Information Services, Employment Skill Banks, Financial Aid. Editor: Willis Johnson. Garrett Park, Md.: Garrett Park Press, 1973.

Directory's four sections cover general employment and educational assistance, federal assistance programs, women's career counseling, college and university awards. Appendix E lists books and reports available for financial aid in dental education; engineering; hotel, restaurant, and institutions; library work; psychology; social work; journalism; law; and business.

Ebony Handbook. Chicago, Ill.: Johnson Publishing Co., 1974.

See *Career Guide* and *Available Scholarships, Fellowships and Loans.*

Equal Employment Opportunity for Minority Group College Graduates: Locating, Recruiting and Employing. Robert Calvert, Jr. Garrett Park, Md.: Garrett Park Press, 1972.

Demographic listing of employment opportunities.

Graduate and Professional School Opportunities for Minority Students. Princeton, N.J.: Educational Testing Service, 1973-74, 5th ed., free.

Covers business schools, law, medicine, dental and others. Graduate programs range from agricultural, art, chemistry, veterinary medicine, zoology. Book is broken down by university listing. Excellent data on applications, tests, number of students accepted and enrollment.

Guide to Financial Aid for Students and Parents. College Entrance Examination Board. Elizabeth Suchar. New York: Simon and Schuster, 1975.

Lists eligibility requirements, how to estimate ability to pay.

Handbook for Careerists. Ruth Bates Harris. Washington, D.C.: U.S. Employment Service.

How to Get Money for Education, Fellowships and Scholarships. Human Resources Network. Radnor, Pa.: Chilton Book Co., 1975.

Fundraising. Broken down into three categories by states. Lists the amounts given and the person to contact. Index of foundations, endowment funds and associations. Lists scholarships available by fields.

Lovejoy's Career and Vocational School Guide: A Source Book, Clue Book and Directory of Institutions Training for Job Opportunities. Clarence E. Lovejoy. New York: Simon and Schuster, 1973.

Arranged alphabetically by profession, state, schools.

Manpower Research and Development Projects. U.S. Dept. of Labor Manpower Administration, 1975.

National Directory of Adult and Continuing Education: A Guide to Programs, Materials and Services for Libraries, Business and Industry, Colleges and Universities, Hospitals, Educational Organizations, Vocational and Technical Schools. Steven E. Goodman. Somerville, N.J.: Education and Training Association, 1968. Address: P.O. Box 370, Somerville, N.J. 08876.

The New York Times Guide to Continuing Education in America. College Entrance Examination Board. Frances Coombs Thomson. New York: The New York Times, 1972.

Correspondence on how to get college credit for what you've learned after school. Includes biography for adult student requirements. Schools are listed in alphabetical order. College Level Examination Program (CLEP) for continuing education.

Scholarships, Fellowships and Loans. S. Norman Feingold. Arlington, Mass.: Bellman Publishing Co., 1972, vol. V.

Student Financial Help: A Guide to Money for College. Louis T. and Joyce W. Scaringi. Garden City, N.Y.: Doubleday & Co., 1974.

Part I covers federal undergraduate student assistance programs under services, nursing, law enforcement, etc. Part II covers non-federal undergraduate assistance programs relating to merit scholarships, journalism, religious, library, dental, among others.

You Can Win a Scholarship. Barron's Educational Series. Woodbury, Mass.: Barron's Educational Series, 1972.

Scholarship lists, sample tests, Scholastic Aptitude Tests in English, social studies, math, science, music, art.

Your Work & Your Career. Bertram L. Linder and Edwin Selzer. New York: William H. Sadlier, 1975.

Covers wages and salaries, unions, careers in service industry, government, business, recreation industries, professions.

General Publications

Admissions Requirements of American Dental Schools. The American Association of Dental Schools, 211 East Chicago Avenue, Chicago, Ill. 60611. Free.

Annual Directory of Engineering College Research and Graduate Study. American Society of Engineering Education, One Dupont Circle, NW, Washington, D.C.

Black Business Men's Association Manual. BBMA, 3840 Crenshaw Blvd., Suite 202, Los Angeles, Cal.

Four Minorities and the Ph.D. Ford Foundation Graduate Fellowships for Blacks, Chicanos, Puerto Ricans and American Indians. 1973. Ford Foundation, Office of Reports. 320 East 43 Street, New York, N.Y. 10017.

Going Right On. Carl E. Drummond. College Entrance Examination Board, 888 Seventh Avenue, New York, N.Y. 10019. Free.

Graduate Programs and Admissions Manual. The Graduate Records Examination Board and The Council of Graduate Schools in the United States, Box 2606, Princeton, N.J. 08540.

Graduate Schools of Social Work. The Council on Social Work Education, 345 East 46 Street, New York, N.Y. 10017. Free.

Graduate Study in Psychology. The American Psychological Association, 1200 Seventeenth St., NW, Washington, D.C. 20036.

Higher Education for Minority Business. U.S. Dept. of Commerce. Office of Minority Business Enterprise, Washington, D.C. 20230.

How to Write Successful Foundation Presentations. Joseph Dermer. New York: Public Materials Center.

Medical School Admission Requirements. Association of American Medical Colleges, One Dupont Circle, NW, Washington, D.C. 20036.

Pre-Law Handbook, Law School Programs, Box 944, Princeton, N.J. 08540.

Selected Bibliography of Grantsmanship. Dan Levitan. Newton, Mass.: Council of Planning Librarians, Exchange Bibliography 641.

A Selected List of Major Fellowship Opportunities and Aids to Advanced Education for United States Citizens. National Academy of Sciences. 2101 Constitution Avenue, NW, Washington, D.C. 20418. Free.

Periodicals

Grantsmanship Center NEWS. 8 issues for $15 per year. 1015 West Olympic Blvd., Los Angeles, Cal. 90015.

Grantsmanship News. A monthly letter on private and federal grants published by the University Resources, Inc., 160 Central Park South, New York, N.Y. 10019.

The Black Scholar. 10 issues for $12 per year. Black World Foundation, P.O. Box 908, Sausalito, Cal. 94965.

Index

Advertising agent, 122
Aeronautical engineer, 84
Air traffic controller, 60, 194
Aircraft supplier, 132
Airline pilot, 12, 30
Alsandor, H. Jude, 112
Anderson, Eddie J., 40
Anderson, Vinton Randolph, 192
Architect, 74, 174
Artist, 110, 124, 206
Assistant principal, 36
Automobile dealer, 184

Bank president, 164
Bishop, 192
Bowers, Mary, 106
Brown, Dorothy Lavinia, 14
Brown, Hezekiah, 150
Brown, Mary Richardson, 116
Brunson, Dorothy Edwards, 72
Bryson, Louis O., 226
Burrell, Berkeley, 156
Burroughs, Margaret, 110
Business school operator, 172
Businessman, 94, 186, 208
Businesswoman, 96
Byer, Erroll, 80

Cable TV administrator, 114
Campbell, Wendell J., 174
Cardiologist, 202
Carroll, Lawrence W., 94
Catering contractor, 22
Certified public accountant, 58
Chappell, (Bill) Will A., 230
Chemist, 214
Childs, John Allen, III, 168
Civic leader, 188

Civil rights specialist, 226
Communications educator, 102
Community activist, 94
Community leader, 78, 106
Concert singer, 42
Conley, Everett Nathaniel, 196
Construction company owner, 170
Contractor, 136, 204
Corporate director, 190
Correction officer, 178
Costello, Deloris, 102
County commissioner, 212
Cummings, Alonza, 60

Darden, Margaret Singleton, 68
Davis, Willie D., 186
Dean, college, 154
Doman, James Richard, Jr., 74
Dramatic artist, 28
Dry cleaning entrepreneur, 156
Duren, Bob D., 108

Early childhood educator, 68
Education administrator, 52
Employee counselor, 66
Employment agent, 70, 228
Equal employment administrator, 152
Ethnomusicologist, 34

Film producer, 144
Fire chief, 98
Flight instructor, 138
Founder of Black Awareness schools, 82
Fuller, Hoyt W., 86
Funeral service director, 168

Galvin-Lewis, Jane, 18
Gaston, Rosetta, 78

Gilliam, Barbara, 158
Government administrator, 46
Graham, Edward T., 212
Grant, Jacquelyn, 64
Groomes, Freddie Lang, 52
Gynecologist, 80

Haig, Theodore Josiah, 36
Hale, Larzette Golden, 58
Hansen, Austin, 20
Harper, Katy Jean, 194
Harris, Ruth Bates, 88
Herbologist, 120
Hicks, William, Jr., 70
Historian, 90
Hollingsworth, Al, 208
Hunton, Benjamin Lacy, 46

Jackson, Hobart C., 146
Jackson, L.B., 132
Janitorial maintenance operator, 198
Jazz musician, 56
Jenkins, Cynthia, 220
Jones, Johnny L., 180
Judge, 130

Kearney, Annette Gaines, 24
Keyes, Robert J., 190
Keys, Brady, Jr., 26
Kinney, Esi Sylvia, 34
Kirven, Joe W., 204

Labor mediator, 150
Lacey, Archie L., 16
Law professor, 50
Layton, William, 152
Lecturer, 206
Legal counsel, 48
Lewis, Edward, 44
Librarian, 220
Lindsey, Claudia, 42
Long, Nate, 128
Lucas, Wm. Larry, 210

McBrown, Gertrude P., 28
McNeil, Dee Dee, 126

Magazine editor, 86
Magazine publisher, 44
Malone, Annie Estelle, 166
Mapp, Edward, 162
Marine operations servicer, 112
Medical educational director, 14
Minister, 212
Montgomery, Catherine Lewis, 188
Moore, Daniel A., 144
Moore, John E., 120
Music communicator, 126, 230

Newspaper editor, 176, 222
Newspaper publisher, 224
Norwood, William, 12
Nutritionist, 120

O'Bryant, Henri, 62
Obstetrician, 80
Opera singer, 42
Owens, Charlene B., 96

Parker, Marjorie Holloman, 134
Pediatrician, 148
Photographer, 20
Physical therapist, 92
Pilot, see Airline pilot
Poet, 196
Police officer, 40
Porter, Charles W., 222
Precision products manufacturer, 142
Preiskel, Barbara Scott, 48
Professor, 134, 162
Psychologist, 24

Radio station manager, 72
Rainey, Charles, III, 56
Rattley, Jessie Menifield, 172
Real estate developer, 216
Record producer, 38
Reed, Phyllis, 122
Reid, Edith C., 202
Religious garment manufacturer, 62
Restaurateur, 70
Restaurant chain owner, 26
Reynolds, Charles M., Jr., 164

Ringgold, Faith, 206
Russell, Nathaniel S., 216

Satterfield, William H., 228
Science educator, 16
Sengstacke, John H., 224
Shern, James H. 98
Shuman, Jerome, 50
Sickle cell researcher, 104
Sinkford, Jeanne Craig, 154
Smith, Ida Van, 138
Smith, J. Clay, Jr., 114
Smith, Vincent, 124
Social gerontologist, 146
Social service director, 166
Space program administrator, 88
Statistician, 210
Superintendent of schools, 180
Syphax, William T., 170

Taylor, Bernardo, 214
Taylor, Roosevelt, 136
Teacher, 206
Teasley, Marie Wright, 176
Television producer, 116, 128
Theologian, 64
Thomas, Tasha, 38
Tilmon, James Alphonso, Sr., 30
Tombs, Leroy C., 22
Tonic, Charles Ronald, 178
Trainer consultant, 18
Travel consultant, 158

Urban planner, 174

Walker, Brenda, 92
Warren, Joseph M., 66
Weathercaster, 30
Wethers, Doris, 148
Whitten, Charles F., 104
Wilks, Gertrude, 82
Williams, Chancellor, 90
Williams, Jesse J., 142
Williams, Nathaniel D., 198
Williams, O.S., 24

Wilson, Porterfield, 184
Women's newspaper editor, 176
Wright, Bruce McM., 130
Writer, 86, 110

Youth program director, 108